1,000
FACTS ABOUT
INSECTS

NANCY HONOVICH   FOREWORD BY BILL LAMP, PROFESSOR OF ENTOMOLOGY

WASHINGTON, D.C.

TABLE OF CONTENTS

6	FOREWORD	54	FADS
8	10 FAST FACTS	56	LOVE BUGS
10	HABITATS	58	MACHINES
12	NUMBER CRUNCHING	60	APPETIZING INSECTS
14	ANTS	62	SOCIETIES
16	SENSES	64	COMMEMORATIVE FACTS
18	AQUATIC INSECTS	66	COMMUNICATION
20	MOTION	68	BLOOD AND GUTS
22	FICTIONAL INSECTS	70	BODY SNATCHERS
24	DISGUISES	72	INVASIONS
26	LIFE CYCLES	74	INSECT-EATERS
28	PREDATORS	76	LIGHTMAKERS
30	FORAGING	78	BUTTERFLIES
32	ARCHITECTS	80	WEIRD INSECTS
34	AT THE EXTREMES	82	ENDANGERED INSECTS
36	GENES	84	BEETLES
38	STINGERS, BITERS, AND BLOODSUCKERS	86	CONSERVATION
40	DEFENSES	88	GLOSSARY
42	BEES	90	KINDS OF INSECTS
44	FORGOTTEN INSECTS	94	INDEX
46	COUSINS	95	RESOURCES
48	FAMILIES	96	CREDITS
50	HELPERS		
52	MIGRATION		

a Costa Rican
leaf mantis

Insects are the most diverse, widespread, and fascinating animals on planet Earth.

We learn more about insects every day because many people, like you, have added to that knowledge. Through the study of insects—entomology—we learn about their many forms and behaviors and the changes that take place in species over generations.

Just about anywhere you travel, insects are part of the ecosystem of life. A short walk in the woods can reveal many insects feeding on plants, foraging on flowers, and hiding under logs. A picnic by a pond is a great place to observe flying insects like dragonflies, as well as many jumping insects along the shore. Around a house or apartment, moths are attracted to porch lights, beetles hide under flowerpots, and katydids sing from the trees. The diversity of insects and the way they live is especially great in tropical regions like Central America and Southeast Asia. These areas are where social ants and termites are active and the largest insects are found. Yet, the cold alpine habitats on mountaintops are great places to see bees and butterflies foraging on wildflowers. In fact, insects are common everywhere on our planet except in open oceans and the frigid polar regions.

All insects have six legs, an exoskeleton, and a head, thorax, and abdomen. Many have wings and are capable of flying. They come in many sizes, shapes, colors, and textures. Why are there so many kinds of insects? The answer is because each one is capable of surviving by adapting to where they live. Some eat plants, some eat decaying plants and animals, and some eat other insects. There are insects that can hide from predators by burrowing underground; others can taste bad to predators or disguise themselves to appear invisible. Scientists have discovered over a million kinds of insects, and they expect there are likely 10 million kinds, each with their own special characteristics and way of living.

Insects are incredibly important to life on our planet. While there are insects that are harmful or eat our food, many more are valuable to us as predators of our pests, as pollinators of our crops, and as decomposers of our dead plants and animals. Insects are important to cultures around the world. They also provide us with important products like silk and honey, and through pollination, the fruits and vegetables that we eat.

This book highlights the diversity and lives of insects. Learn about their adaptations to extreme conditions, their ability to perceive and move about their habitat, and even how insect predators attack their prey. There is lots to learn about insects here, yet so much more waiting to be discovered!

When asked why I study insects, I often say because I find them amazing. I see beauty in all insects. Certainly we can all share our appreciation of the beauty of butterflies and dragonflies, but every species has a unique form and function that I find fascinating. The discovery of these forms and functions is endless, and through scientific inquiry, we can understand the diversity of insects and their importance to our lives. *1,000 Facts About Insects* will help you discover amazing facts about both the insects you encounter in your daily life and those that live across the world.

BILL LAMP
Professor of Entomology,
University of Maryland

swallowtail butterfly caterpillar (*Papilio machaon*)

10 FAST FACTS

1
INSECTS ARE SMALL ANIMALS THAT HAVE A HARD **OUTER SKELETON** CALLED AN **EXOSKELETON.**

2
All insect bodies are made up of three parts: a head, a middle section called the thorax, and a rear section called the abdomen.

head   thorax   abdomen

3
An insect's head has EYES and two ANTENNAE, which can be used to touch and smell.

4
CONNECTED TO THE THORAX ARE AN INSECT'S WINGS AND SIX LEGS.

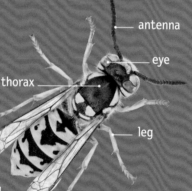

antenna

eye

thorax

leg

wing

5
ALL INSECTS BELONG TO A GROUP CALLED ARTHROPODS. THE WORD MEANS "JOINTED FOOT" IN GREEK, AND REFERS TO THE INSECTS' JOINTED LEGS.

6
Although most insects have **ONE OR TWO PAIRS OF WINGS,** some species cannot use their WINGS to fly.

ABOUT INSECTS

7 Insects can have **SIMPLE EYES,** which have a single lens, or **COMPOUND EYES,** which have many lenses.

8 Some insects, such as **CICADAS, HAVE SIMPLE AND COMPOUND EYES.** The simple eyes see light and dark. Compound eyes create images and are used to see the world around them.

9 All bugs are insects, but NOT ALL INSECTS ARE BUGS.

10 TRUE BUGS ARE INSECTS THAT HAVE MOUTHPARTS FOR SUCKING UP LIQUID, SUCH AS **PLANT SAP** OR **BLOOD.**

leafcutter ants taking leaf fragments to their colony

INSECT HABITATS

spotted fritillary butterfly

Mountains

Mountains are rocky regions that become colder as the height above sea level increases. The amount of oxygen in the air also decreases with elevation. **Some insects you'll find:** black eye grasshopper, spotted fritillary butterfly, alpine bumblebee

yellow-fronted bumblebee

Tundra

The tundra is a large treeless region where temperatures can drop way below freezing—32°F (0°C). **Some insects you'll find:** yellow-fronted bumblebee, ice crawler, jutta arctic butterfly

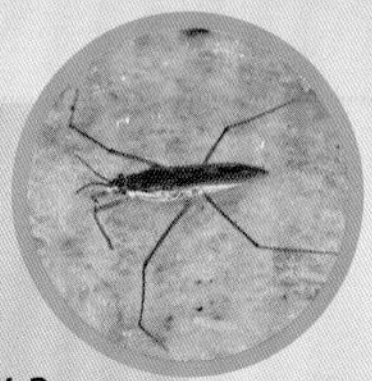

Oceans and seas

These bodies of salt water cover 75 percent of the Earth's surface. Only a tiny number of insects make the sea their home. **Some insects you'll find:** water skater, sea skater, *Clunio marinus* midge, *Pontomyia* Edwards midge

water skater

tok-tokkie beetle

Hot and cold deserts

Deserts are large areas that receive less than 10 inches (25 cm) of rainfall each year. **Some insects you'll find:** tok-tokkie beetle, Saharan desert ant, antarctic midge, swallowtail butterfly

NORTH AMERICA

ATLANTIC OCEAN

PACIFIC OCEAN

SOUTH AMERICA

E

Urban areas

Built-up areas, or cities, are places where the living conditions—and food supplies—are largely influenced and controlled by human activity. **Some insects you'll find:** common bedbug, pavement ant, German cockroach

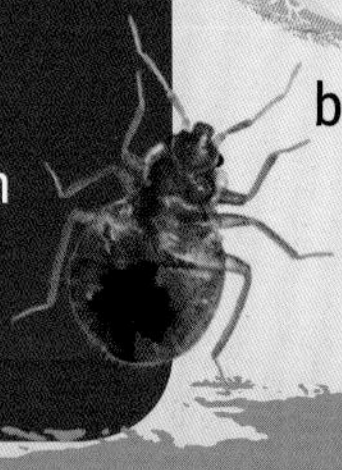

bedbug

grasshopper

Grasslands

Grasslands are flat, open areas with wild grasses and few trees. **Some insects you'll find:** grasshopper, robber fly, velvet ant, plant-hopper

ANTA

Insects can be found in a variety of habitats all around the world, from the icy tundra to scorching deserts and from tropical rain forests to aquatic environments. Insects can be found even in your own backyard.

KEY

- Mountains
- Oceans and seas
- Tundra
- Temperate forests
- Urban areas
- Grasslands
- Rivers and streams
- Tropical rain forests
- Ponds, lakes, and swamps
- Hot and cold deserts
- Other forests

OCEAN

bark-gnawing beetle

Other forests
Northern forests have conifer trees with needle leaves. Some forests are open areas.

EUROPE

ASIA

AFRICA

PACIFIC

OCEAN

monarch butterfly

Temperate forests
Temperate forests have tall trees with broad leaves, and each year experience four climate seasons. **Some insects you'll find:** monarch butterfly, striped hawkmoth, sassafras borer

INDIAN

OCEAN

jewel beetle

Tropical rain forests
These huge expanses of trees get more than 100 inches (254 cm) of rainfall each year. Tropical rain forests lie near Earth's Equator. **Some insects you'll find:** jewel beetle, giant rainforest mantis, postman butterfly

AUSTRALIA

caddisfly larva

Rivers and streams
Rivers and streams are moving bodies of water that vary in their amount of water through the year. **Some insects you'll find:** caddisfly, stonefly, midge

mayfly

Ponds, lakes, and swamps
These bodies of standing water have little salt and many aquatic plants. **Some insects you'll find:** mayfly, dragonfly, damselfly

RCTICA

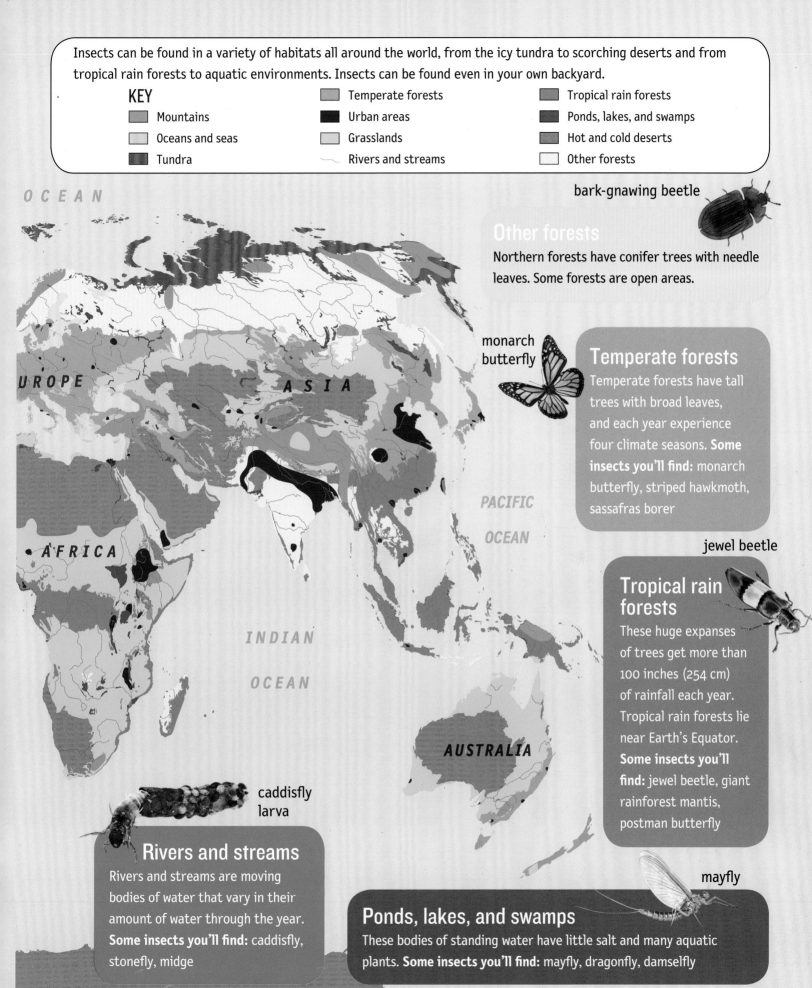

1 There are about **1,000,000** known insect species in the world.

2 Scientists suspect that up to **30 MILLION** insect species have **YET TO BE DISCOVERED.**

3 About 85,000 of all known insects are **TRUE BUGS.** They include **STINK BUGS, GIANT WATER BUGS,** and **BEDBUGS.**

4 THERE ARE 825 KNOWN **tick** SPECIES. SOME TICKS CAN SURVIVE AS LONG AS 200 DAYS **without food or water.**

5 With at least **90,000** INSECT SPECIES, BRAZIL has more insect diversity than anywhere else in the world.

25 NUMBER-CRUNCHING

6 Americans share **their homes** with more than 500 species of **arthropods** at any given time. These include flies, cockroaches, moths, and spiders.

7 Scientists estimate that there are 90 million **MITES** in every acre (0.4 ha) of **SOIL** just in North Carolina, U.S.A.

8 ABOUT 120,000 SPECIES OF **DIPTERANS,** OR "TRUE FLIES," ARE **BUZZING** AROUND EARTH. THESE INCLUDE FRUIT FLIES, HOUSE FLIES, AND CRANE FLIES.

9 MOSQUITOES ARE ALSO CONSIDERED DIPTERANS. THEY MAKE UP ABOUT **3,500 SPECIES** OF THE GROUP.

10 More than 2,000 **FLEA** species have been identified. Fortunately for Fido, only a few of these species ATTACK DOGS.

11 There are about **10 million billion ants** in the world. There are only **7 billion people.**

12 CATERPILLARS ARE NOT WORMS BUT INSECTS—THEY ARE THE **LARVAL,** OR YOUNG, STAGE OF BUTTERFLIES, MOTHS, AND SKIPPERS. SOME GROW TO MORE THAN FOUR INCHES (10 CM) LONG.

13

The AMAZON RAIN FOREST is home to more than 100,000 animal species. At least 90 PERCENT of these species are insects.

14

There are at least 1,800 EARWIG species. Despite popular belief, not one of these species lays eggs in HUMAN EARS.

15

AS YOU READ THIS, ABOUT 4,000 COCKROACH SPECIES ARE SCUTTLING ACROSS THE GLOBE.

16

About 2,500 MAYFLY species have been identified. Many of these insects will die only a few hours AFTER BECOMING ADULTS.

17

BEETLES ARE THE MOST DIVERSE GROUP OF INSECTS. MORE THAN 400,000 SPECIES HAVE BEEN DISCOVERED.

18

The least diverse order of insects is the ROCK CRAWLERS. Only 25 SPECIES are known.

FACTS ABOUT INSECTS

19

All 5,000 dragonfly species have KNIFELIKE TEETH. They belong to an order of insects called Odonata, which means "TOOTHED ONE."

20

About 400 insect species belong to the order Embiodea, or WEB SPINNERS. These insects can SPIN SILK in both adult and immature stages of life.

21

THERE ARE 2,750 TERMITE SPECIES IN THE WORLD. THEY EAT 24 HOURS A DAY, 7 DAYS A WEEK.

22

SPINELESS ANIMALS, together known as INVERTEBRATES, make up 95.6 percent of the animal kingdom. Of these, 71.1 PERCENT are insects.

23

MORE THAN 155,000 SPECIES OF BUTTERFLIES, MOTHS, AND SKIPPERS ARE FLUTTERING AROUND THE WORLD.

24

There are 5,500 species of BOOK LICE and BARK LICE. These insects aren't actually lice. But like lice, they are very small and HARD TO SEE.

25

There are about 200 MILLION INSECTS for every HUMAN ON EARTH.

1
Ants are social insects. They live together in groups called colonies.

2
An ant queen produces eggs, male ants mate with the queen, and female workers provide food and protect the colony.

3
Yellow crazy ants can form supercolonies that contain many nests and queens.

4
In 2001, a supercolony of billions of yellow crazy ants was found on Christmas Island.

5
Ants can be found on every continent on Earth except Antarctica.

6
Scientists estimate that ants have been around for about 130 million years.

7
Waste produced by ants—as well as by other insects—is called frass.

8
Black garden ants don't leave their waste lying around. Instead, they move it to "toilet" areas in the nest.

9
A trap-jaw ant can shut its jaws at 145 miles an hour (233 km/h). That's 2,300 times faster than a human eye blinks.

10
Turtle ant soldiers use their heads to block entrances to their nest. This helps defend the nest from intruders.

11
An Asian weaver ant was recorded holding a 500-milligram (about .02-ounce) weight. That's 100 times the ant's body weight.

12
Carpenter ants use their mouthparts to chew holes into wood. They build their nests inside these holes.

13
Worker ants of the *Carebara atoma* species are so tiny they can be difficult to see even under a microscope.

14
One of the largest known ant species is the giant forest ant. Adults can reach lengths of 1.2 inches (30 mm).

15
Weaver ants create leafy nests in trees located in Africa, Asia, and Australia.

16
Weaver ant larvae secrete a sticky substance. Adult weaver ants use the substance as glue to seal nest leaves together.

17
During a flood in South Carolina, U.S.A., fire ants were seen linking their legs and mouthparts together to form a raft.

18
Although a male black garden ant lives for only a few weeks, the queen can live up to 30 years.

19
A team of U.S. scientists is creating a website called Antweb that will feature 3-D images of every known ant species.

20
Some ants of the genus *Pheidole* inject their larvae with a hormone that turns them into giant super-soldiers to defend the colony.

21
As leafcutter ants travel through a forest searching for leaves, they leave behind a scent trail. This helps the ants keep track of their path.

22
The ant *Temnothorax longispinosus* can recognize its enemies—particularly those that threaten the lives of its colony members.

23
When an Asian needle ant finds a snack that's too large to carry, it returns to its nest to grab a worker ant to help move the load.

24
An ant queen can lay up to 300,000 eggs in a span of a few days.

25
Lemon ants, which live in the Amazon rain forest, will build nests only in trees of the species *Duroia hirsute*.

26
Because the ants thrive on the *Duroia hirsute* tree, they kill all other tree species by injecting them with a deadly acid.

27
When *Temnothorax unifasciatus* ants get sick, they leave their nests to die.

28
To protect their queen, workers of the army ant *Eciton burchellii* will interlock their bodies to create a shelter.

29
The shelters created by *Eciton burchellii* can consist of up to 700,000 ants and can measure three feet (0.9 m) across.

30
Ants of the genus *Dorymyrmex* have been known to climb on top of seed-harvester ants to lick their bodies and mouthparts clean.

31
After acacia ants eat nectar from Central America's acacia trees, they become forever unable to digest nectar from any other tree species.

32
In exchange for the nectar, the acacia ants will defend the trees from other animals and weeds that try to feed from them.

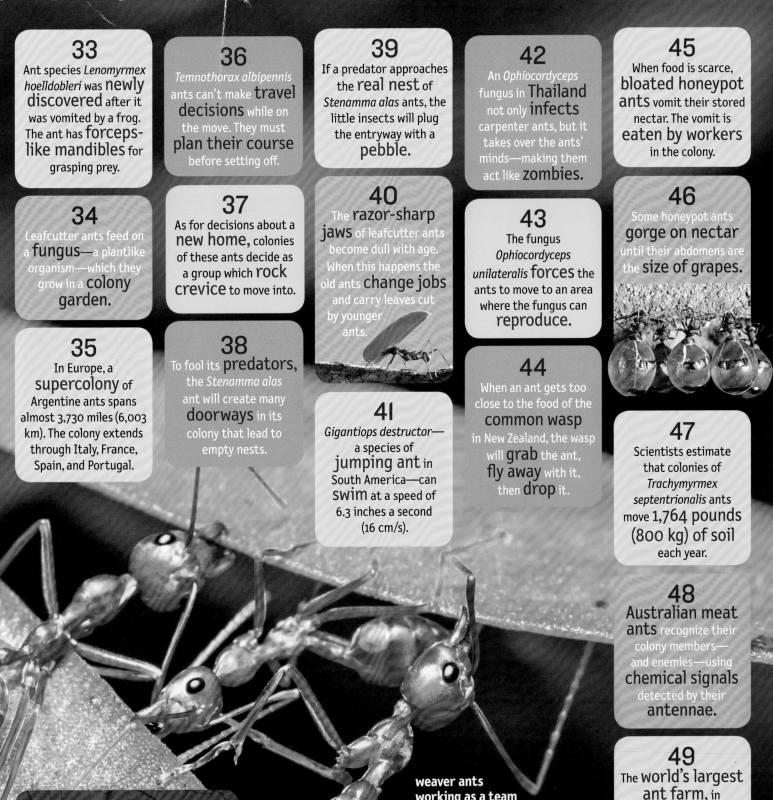

33
Ant species *Lenomyrmex hoelldobleri* was newly discovered after it was vomited by a frog. The ant has forceps-like mandibles for grasping prey.

36
Temnothorax albipennis ants can't make travel decisions while on the move. They must plan their course before setting off.

39
If a predator approaches the real nest of *Stenamma alas* ants, the little insects will plug the entryway with a pebble.

42
An *Ophiocordyceps* fungus in Thailand not only infects carpenter ants, but it takes over the ants' minds—making them act like zombies.

45
When food is scarce, bloated honeypot ants vomit their stored nectar. The vomit is eaten by workers in the colony.

34
Leafcutter ants feed on a fungus—a plantlike organism—which they grow in a colony garden.

37
As for decisions about a new home, colonies of these ants decide as a group which rock crevice to move into.

40
The razor-sharp jaws of leafcutter ants become dull with age. When this happens the old ants change jobs and carry leaves cut by younger ants.

43
The fungus *Ophiocordyceps unilateralis* forces the ants to move to an area where the fungus can reproduce.

46
Some honeypot ants gorge on nectar until their abdomens are the size of grapes.

35
In Europe, a supercolony of Argentine ants spans almost 3,730 miles (6,003 km). The colony extends through Italy, France, Spain, and Portugal.

38
To fool its predators, the *Stenamma alas* ant will create many doorways in its colony that lead to empty nests.

41
Gigantiops destructor—a species of jumping ant in South America—can swim at a speed of 6.3 inches a second (16 cm/s).

44
When an ant gets too close to the food of the common wasp in New Zealand, the wasp will grab the ant, fly away with it, then drop it.

47
Scientists estimate that colonies of *Trachymyrmex septentrionalis* ants move 1,764 pounds (800 kg) of soil each year.

48
Australian meat ants recognize their colony members—and enemies—using chemical signals detected by their antennae.

49
The world's largest ant farm, in Singapore, is the size of a small bed mattress.

50
A *Thaumatomyrmex* ant has pitchfork-like mandibles. During an attack, the ant can retract its mandibles to form a face guard.

weaver ants working as a team to make a nest

50 Amazing Facts About ANTS

15

1 Bees can see blue, green, violet, orange, and yellow. But they are unable to see the color red.

2 Fruit flies have **temperature receptors** that help them sense if their surroundings are **too hot or too cold.**

3 Butterflies have receptors on their **antennae** that help them **smell odors** such as the scent of honey given off by nectar.

domino cockroach

4 Cockroaches have hairs called setae that help them sense a **change in air pressure.** This helps the insects escape **approaching predators such as humans.**

5 A species of **midge** that flies in **complete darkness** was recently discovered **in a cave.** Scientists suspect the insect uses its forelegs to feel its way around.

6 Some grasshoppers **hear** with an **organ on their abdomen** called a **tympanum.**

7 A **thin membrane** on each of a cricket's **front legs** works like an **eardrum** to help the insect hear.

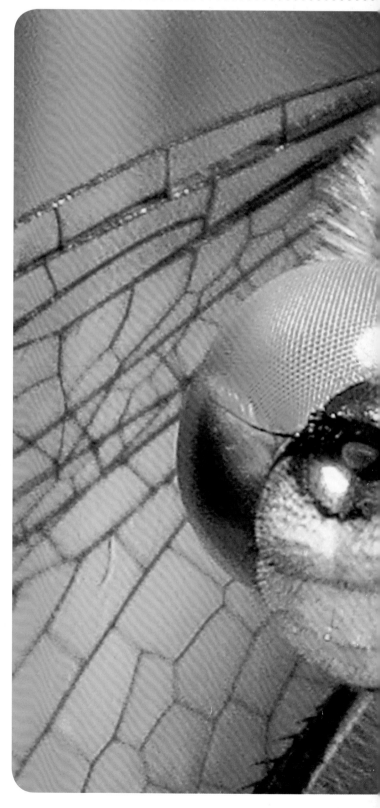

INSECT SENSES

8 Dragonflies have the largest compound eyes of any insect. Each eye contains up to 30,000 lenses, which help the insects see in all directions.

9 Mosquitoes rely partly on their sense of smell to find humans to bite. They can smell carbon dioxide—the gas that humans breathe out.

10 Flies use the bristles that cover their mouthparts, legs, and wings to taste food.

11 Studies show that the blue morpho butterfly uses its wings to hear low-pitched sounds, like the flapping wings of an insect-hungry bird.

12 Bog orchids rely on mosquitoes for pollination. So they give off a humanlike body odor that attracts mosquitoes.

13 Fire-chaser beetles, which lay their eggs in freshly burnt trees, have pits beneath their middle legs that help them detect heat.

14 Ants have an excellent sense of taste. They can taste the difference between sour, sweet, bitter, and salty flavors.

15 Although caterpillars have six simple eyes, their vision is poor. They use sense organs in their mouths to find food.

eyes of a dragonfly

1 A WATER STRIDER'S HAIRY LEGS trap air. This helps the insect FLOAT ON WATER.

2 THE WATER STRIDER'S MIDDLE LEGS PROPEL THE INSECT FORWARD, WHILE ITS HIND LEGS ACT LIKE A RUDDER. IT USES ITS FRONT LEGS TO SNATCH PREY.

3 Water striders can stay afloat while carrying 15 TIMES THEIR OWN WEIGHT.

4 MAYFLIES LAY THEIR EGGS IN FRESHWATER. THE FULLY GROWN NYMPHS MAKE THEIR WAY TO THE WATER'S SURFACE OR SHORELINE.

5 WHIRLIGIG BEETLES have SPLIT EYES for seeing above and beneath the water's surface.

25 SPLASHY FACTS ABOUT

6 THE great diving beetle CARRIES A bubble of air WHEN IT TRAVELS BENEATH THE WATER'S SURFACE, USING IT to breathe.

7 A midge larva—called a BLOODWORM—lives in MUDDY PONDS AND STREAMS, where breathable oxygen supplies are low.

8 To breathe, bloodworms rely on a protein in their blood called HEMOGLOBIN, which holds a SUPPLY OF OXYGEN.

9 Some caddisfly larvae MAKE SILK NETS TO CATCH ALGAE and other food suspended in water.

10 MANY STONEFLIES AND CADDISFLIES HAVE gills on their thorax OR ABDOMEN. GILLS ALLOW BREATHING IN WATER.

11 SMALL MINNOW MAYFLIES CLING TO ROCK SURFACES AND SWIM SWIFTLY FROM ONE ROCK TO ANOTHER.

12 Dragonfly nymphs have GILLS INSIDE THEIR BODIES.

13 To ESCAPE PREDATORS, dragonfly nymphs can contract their abdomens and EXPEL JETS OF WATER. This thrusts the insects forward.

14 Most mosquitoes LAY EGGS in just about ANY BODY OF STANDING OR SLOW-MOVING WATER. This includes everything from a pond to your pet's water bowl.

15 MOSQUITO LARVAE HAVE HOLLOW BREATHING TUBES LIKE SNORKELS. THE TUBES REACH TO THE WATER'S SURFACE.

16 The open end of the mosquito's breathing tube is lined with WATERPROOF HAIRS. When the mosquito dives deep into the water, the hairs press together to keep water out.

17 Stonefly larvae are SENSITIVE TO WATER POLLUTION. Environmental experts can look to these insects for information about water quality.

AQUATIC INSECTS

18 ADULT DIVING BEETLES CAN EAT LARGE PREY SUCH AS WORMS AND FISH. THEY HOLD THE PREY WITH THEIR LEGS AND TEAR IT TO PIECES WITH THEIR MOUTHPARTS.

19 Male diving beetles use their "SUCTION CUP" HAIRS to latch on to female beetles underwater.

20 Water scorpions have long TAILS. When submerged in water, they use these tails as SNORKELS TO BREATHE.

21 ALTHOUGH MANY INSECT SPECIES LIVE NEAR COASTLINES, FIVE SPECIES FROM A SEA SKATER FAMILY LIVE IN THE OPEN OCEAN.

22 Scientists have discovered that some sea skaters have been LAYING THEIR EGGS on a LARGE PATCH OF PLASTIC GARBAGE in the Pacific Ocean.

23 BRINE FLY LARVAE have special organs that REMOVE EXTRA SALT from their bodies.

24 AFTER ADULT BRINE FLIES EMERGE FROM THEIR UNDERWATER CASINGS, THEY SURROUND THEMSELVES IN AN AIR BUBBLE AND FLOAT TO THE WATER'S SURFACE.

25 The backswimmer gets its name because it SWIMS UPSIDE DOWN on its back.

15 SWIFT AND BOUNCY

❶ An adult common froghopper is only 0.2 inch (5 mm) long, but it **can jump a whopping 28 inches (71 cm)** into the air.

❷ The secret to the froghopper's leaping ability lies in its **hind legs,** which **work like catapults** to launch the tiny insect.

❸ Flies are difficult to **swat** because they are far more **aerodynamic** and **maneuverable** in the air than any airplane or helicopter. They can twist, turn, and reach full flying speed in 1/50 of a second.

❹ To test a **horse fly's speed,** a scientist fired a plastic pellet from an air rifle. The fly zipped after the pellet and caught it midair.

❺ The scientist estimated that the horse fly flew at 90 miles an hour (145 km/h). That's **as fast as a speeding car.**

❻ An adult tiger beetle can run five miles an hour (8 km/h)—so fast that it **temporarily blinds itself** in the process.

❼ **Mexican jumping beans** get their bouncing abilities from a **moth larva** developing inside each bean.

8 The tiger beetle covers **120 body lengths a second.** To match this speed, champion racer Usain Bolt would have to run 480 miles an hour (772 km/h).

9 When the *Cephalotes atratus* ant falls from its treetop home in South and Central America, it **glides safely** to a lower part of the tree.

10 To slow its fall, the *Cephalotes atratus* ant **splays its legs** out in a **parachute-like** way.

11 The globe skimmer is a dragonfly that can travel **thousands of miles.** Beating its wings takes a lot of energy, so the insect **relies on the wind** to carry it.

12 Tiny midges known as no-see-ums can **beat their wings** about **1,000 times a second.**

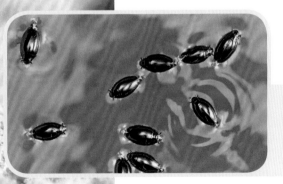

13 Thanks partly to its oar-shaped middle and hind legs, the whirligig beetle can **zip across the water** in bursts of 39 inches a second (99 cm/s).

14 Fleas have a springlike mechanism in their hind legs that helps them **leap 200 times their body length.**

15 Some aircraft pilots have reported seeing **monarch butterflies** flying **as high as 11,000 feet (3,353 m)** above the ground.

An adult tiger beetle. These beetles hold the record for the fastest runner.

1 *Bee Movie* tells the story of a young **male bee** whose job is to **make honey.** In reality, male bees have only one job: to **mate with the queen.**

2 In *Bee Movie*, the voice of **Mooseblood the mosquito** is provided by Chris Rock, a comedian who also voiced **Marty the zebra** in *Madagascar*.

3 In the movie *A Bug's Life,* Flik the ant assembles a **group of warrior bugs** to fight a band of grasshoppers.

4 Flik's group of warrior bugs includes a **black widow spider named Rose.** However, **spiders are not bugs, nor insects.** They are arachnids.

5 *A Bug's Life* was inspired partly by **The Ant and the Grasshopper,** a fable by Aesop—a Greek storyteller who lived more than 2,000 years ago.

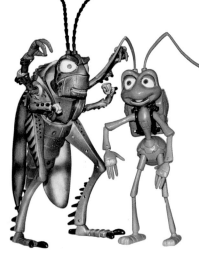

6 In The Ant and the Grasshopper, **a lazy grasshopper makes fun of a hardworking ant** for collecting food to eat during the winter.

7 In the movie *Pinocchio*, Jiminy Cricket appears to have only four legs. **Crickets**— like all insects—actually **have six legs.**

Jiminy Cricket and Pinocchio

FICTIONAL INSECTS

8 In the book *James and the Giant Peach,* by Roald Dahl, a young boy befriends a variety of critters, including a **grasshopper,** a **ladybug,** and a **glowworm.**

9 Tiny comic-book superhero **Ant-Man** has the **ability to communicate with ants** using pheromones and electrical signals.

39 u s a

The Very Hungry Caterpillar
2006

10 *The Very Hungry Caterpillar,* by Eric Carle, is a picture book about a red-faced caterpillar with a big appetite. It has been translated into **62 languages,** including **Urdu, Somali,** and **Icelandic.**

11 The main character in Eric Carle's story was **originally a worm.** Carle's editor thought that a caterpillar would be more interesting, so Carle changed it.

12 In the movie *WALL-E,* Hal the cockroach eats a snack called Kremies. In reality, **cockroaches will eat anything** from meats and sweets to books and hair.

13 **Hal the cockroach** has also made appearances in other movies, including *Ratatouille* and *Wreck-It Ralph.*

14 In the movie *Antz,* **Barbatus** is named after *Pogonomyrmex barbatus*—a **red harvester ant.**

15 Other characters in *Antz* are also inspired by **real ant species.** Colonel Cutter is a leafcutter ant, while Corporal Weaver is a weaver ant.

1 Many insects have CZVORS, PATTERNS, and SHAPES that help them blend in with their surroundings. This characteristic is called CAMOUFLAGE.

2 The adults of many katydid species are BRIGHT GREEN. The color helps the insects BLEND IN with the plants they feed on and STAY HIDDEN from predators.

3 Peppered moth adults have a black-and-white MOTTLED APPEARANCE that helps them GO UNNOTICED when they're resting on tree bark.

4 During the 1800s, to blend in with trees made darker with soot from factories, once light-colored peppered moths evolved to be darker.

5 Some lacewing larvae prey on woolly alder aphids and DISGUISE THEMSELVES by using the victim's woolly wax covering to make a WOOLLY COAT.

25 DECEPTIVE FACTS ABOUT INSECT

6 MIMICRY IN NATURE IS WHEN ONE LIVING THING LOOKS LIKE ANOTHER LIVING THING. MANY INSECTS USE MIMICRY TO SURVIVE IN THE WILD.

7 The adult WALKING STICK INSECT, which looks like a twig, uses mimicry to help it BLEND IN with woodland areas and forests.

8 The largest known walking stick insect—*Phobaeticus kirbyi*, found in Borneo—measures 21 INCHES (53 CM) LONG with its legs stretched out.

9 An adult leaf-litter mantid looks like a DECOMPOSING LEAF on the forest floor and uses this disguise to help it AMBUSH PREY.

10 THE LYGODIUM SPIDER MOTH HAS MARKINGS ON ITS WINGS THAT LOOK LIKE SPINDLY SPIDER LEGS.

11 Thorn bugs, which gather together on PLANT STALKS, look a lot like ROSE THORNS.

12 A THORN BUG'S "THORN" IS REALLY A PRONOTUM, A HARDENED PLATE ON TOP OF THE INSECT'S THORAX.

13 TREEHOPPERS are insects with unusually shaped pronota that resemble anything from ants and fungi to LEAVES and ANTLERS.

14 The **ORCHID MANTIS** is hard to find. This pink-and-white insect has **PETAL-SHAPED LEGS,** giving it the appearance of the flower it hunts from.

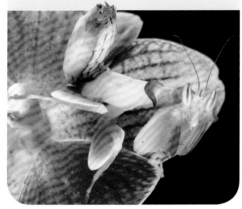

15 When an **OWL BUTTERFLY** is threatened, it lifts its wings to reveal **TWO GIANT EYESPOTS** that resemble the eyes of a much bigger creature—**AN OWL**.

16 **SONGBIRDS** OFTEN FEED ON OWL BUTTERFLIES, BUT IF THEY SEE THE INSECTS' EYESPOTS, THEY ARE REMINDED OF THEIR OWN OWL **PREDATORS** AND KEEP AWAY.

17 Caterpillars of moth species *Apochima juglansiaria* are black and white. When they bend their bodies they look like piles of **BIRD DROPPINGS,** keeping predators away.

18 A species of hover fly resembles **BUMBLEBEE DRONES.** Since some predators know that bumblebees have **STINGERS,** they avoid the hover fly.

DISGUISES

19 The hover fly *Eristalis tenax* takes its disguise one step further by producing sounds made by bumblebees.

20 The wings of the Canada thistle gall fly *Urophora cardui* are transparent with **W-SHAPED MARKINGS.** When the wings are folded, the fly resembles a **SPIDER.**

21 The spicebush swallowtail caterpillar has two large eyespots that give it a **SNAKELIKE APPEARANCE.**

22 Each of the caterpillar's eyespots has a large, black, **PUPIL-LIKE CIRCLE** and a smaller white circle that looks like a **REFLECTION.**

23 The lichen katydid is hard to spot, even when it's moving. This insect's **COLOR** and **SPINES** perfectly match the lichen on which it lives.

24 A blue butterfly caterpillar tricks red ants into believing that it's one of them by **EMITTING A CHEMICAL** that smells just like the ants.

25 The caterpillar then produces the same **SOUND** made by the red ant queen. The ants bring the caterpillar back to their **NEST** and care for it as they would a **QUEEN.**

25

15 FANTASTIC FACTS ABOUT

1 The life cycle of insect species varies. Some mayfly adults live for less than 24 hours while some adult termites may live for 50 years.

2 An insect goes through changes called metamorphosis as it matures. Metamorphosis can be either simple, which includes three stages, or complete, which includes four stages.

3 Most insects hatch from eggs, but some are born live. One type of adult aphid known as a stem mother produces live young.

4 After hatching from its egg, an insect grows until its outer layer, or exoskeleton, becomes too tight. Then it sheds its old exoskeleton in a process called molting and grows a new one.

5 As a mayfly grows into an adult, it can molt 45 times.

6 The stages of simple metamorphosis are egg, nymph, and adult. Grasshoppers and true bugs go through simple metamorphosis.

7 Nymphs, which are immature insects, generally look like miniature versions of adults.

INSECT LIFE CYCLES

8 Some cicadas **can remain nymphs for 17 years.** During this time, the nymph attaches itself to a tree root and **sucks tree sap** for nourishment.

9 The **stages of complete metamorphosis** are **egg, larva, pupa,** and **adult.** Insects such as butterflies and beetles go through complete metamorphosis.

10 An insect **larva** is a **juvenile** that **looks nothing like** its adult stage.

11 A butterfly or moth larva is called a **caterpillar,** a fly larva is a **maggot,** and a beetle larva is a **grub.**

12 Larvae of insects such as alderflies have a sharp organ called an egg burster that they use to crack their shells when they hatch.

13 The **diets** of a larva and adult of an insect species **are often very different.** For example, while adult female mosquitoes **suck blood,** the larvae eat microorganisms such as single-cell algae and bacteria.

14 As a **caterpillar** prepares to enter its pupal stage, it **creates a cocoon made from silk strands.** The silk is produced by **glands** near the caterpillar's mouth.

An adult swallowtail butterfly emerges from its pupa.

15 During the **pupal stage,** almost the **entire body** of the caterpillar **breaks down.** Over time, the pupa develops into an adult.

27

75 ATTACKING FACTS ABOUT INSECT PREDATORS

1 Robber flies attack their prey—mostly bees and wasps—in mid-flight. They swoop down on their victims and inject them with paralyzing saliva.

2 When on a spider's web, the thread-legged bug pretends to be caught. When the spider attempts to feed on the bug, the spider becomes the meal.

3 A single millipede assassin bug nymph isn't powerful enough to kill a millipede. So it works with other nymphs to do the job.

4 Tiger beetle larvae burrow into the ground and hide with jaws open wide. When insect prey scuttle by, they leap out and take a bite.

5 Some *Epomis* beetle larvae have turned the tables on their amphibian attackers. They pounce on frogs and toads and eat them alive!

6 Species of bee assassin bugs coat their legs with sticky plant sap. When a bee approaches, the bugs use their sticky legs to grab it.

7 PRAYING MANTID NYMPHS HAVE BEEN KNOWN TO EAT THEIR OWN SIBLINGS.

8 An eastern yellow jacket adult chews up other insects into a fine paste. It then feeds the paste to its hungry larvae.

9 Mantids turn their heads 180 degrees to scan their surroundings for insect prey.

10 A neon cuckoo bee invades the nest of a blue-banded bee and kills the host's eggs. The neon cuckoo bee then deposits its own eggs into the nest.

11 To snatch its insect prey, a giant darner dragonfly uses its labium. The extendable jaw underneath its head shoots forward and grabs the victim.

12 A praying mantis uses its spine-covered front legs to pierce and pin a struggling creature in place to eat.

13 USING ITS GIANT MANDIBLES, AN ASIAN GIANT HORNET CAN KILL AS MANY AS 20 BEES IN A MINUTE.

14 Unlike most dragonflies, which hunt while flying, Kirby's dropwing skimmer waits on a perch. When it sees prey, it darts out to grab it.

15 Cicada killer wasps plunge their venom-packed stingers into their prey to quickly paralyze them.

16 Spiderwebs are an all-you-can-eat buffet for helicopter damselflies. These insects feed on spiders and other creatures trapped in their webs.

17 When predators try to chomp on an ironclad beetle, they get a surprise. The beetle's tough exoskeleton is almost impossible to bite through.

18 One assassin bug species stabs its ant prey, sucks them dry, and then attaches their corpses to its back for camouflage or as armor.

19 If a male damselfly believes its opponent's wings are more transparent than its own, it doesn't fight for females as the opponent is probably stronger.

A spider wraps up its insect prey.

20 There's a good reason why the green lacewing larva is nicknamed the "aphid lion." It eats as many as 600 aphids during this life stage, which lasts up to three weeks.

21 A DRAGONFLY CAN SNATCH A FRUIT FLY MIDAIR WITHIN ABOUT HALF A SECOND OF LOCATING IT.

22 *Photuris* fireflies imitate the light signals of other firefly species in order to attract, kill, and eat them.

23 The saddleback caterpillar is covered with spines that inject venom into any creature that brushes against it.

24 The larva of a *Hyposmocoma molluscivora* moth traps a snail in silk webbing and then crawls inside the snail's shell to eat it alive.

25 The *Ampulex dementor* wasp is a fierce predator whose name is inspired by the soul-sucking creatures of Harry Potter.

26 This wasp injects its cockroach prey with venom that puts the critter in a zombie-like state.

27 Female velvet ants have been known to plunge their long, needlelike stinger into lizards that try to attack them.

28 THE TARANTULA HAWK IS A SPIDER WASP THAT FEEDS ON ... TARANTULAS.

29 Some tarantula hawks will crawl beneath a tarantula and sting it. Others will grab the tarantula by a rear leg, flip it over, and then sting it.

30 A *Manticora* beetle uses its huge jaws to rip apart its insect or spider prey.

31 CLICK BEETLES STARTLE THEIR PREDATORS BY CATAPULTING INTO THE AIR.

32 A water strider species in Thailand stuns its prey with a bite. One scientist who was bitten by the bug reported pain for 30 minutes.

33 Jack jumper ants leap at attackers. The ants, which are about 0.4 inch (1 cm) long, can cover 10 times their body length in a single leap.

34 To capture prey, ants of the species *Allomerus decemarticulatus* in South America's Amazon rain forest emerge from holes beneath a trap they've created from plant fibers and fungus.

35 The ants pounce on their prey, stretch it out across the trap, then an individual in the group stings it.

36 Research shows that dragonflies have more than a 95 percent success rate in capturing their prey midair.

37 An adult female *Anoplius infuscatus* wasp feeds a spider to its young. After stinging a spider, the wasp can carry it for several minutes until reaching its burrow.

38 The female wasp may cut off the legs of the spider before sealing it in the burrow with her eggs.

39 Western predatory mites are naturally opaque white. But for 24 hours after feeding, they take on the color of their prey.

40 The brown marmorated stink bug lets out a foul-smelling odor when attacked. The odor comes from a smelly chemical produced in the bug's abdomen.

41 Termites have a gunlike snout from which they shoot a deadly glue when threatened.

42 Bulldog ants seize small enemies with large, strong mandibles and then sting them.

43 Giant water bugs—which can grow to 4.7 inches (12 cm) long—can eat small fish, snakes, and baby turtles.

44 Despite their name, Africanized "killer" bees feed on nectar and pollen. The bees are preyed on by various mites.

45 These bees get their killer reputation because they form swarms that viciously attack people and animals that get too close to their territory.

46 PREDATORS THAT GET SICK FROM EATING THE HAWKMOTH CATERPILLAR OFTEN LEARN TO AVOID IT IN THE FUTURE. THEY REMEMBER THE CATERPILLAR BY ITS RED AND BLACK "WARNING" COLORS.

47 Syrphid fly larvae are blind, so they must feel plant surfaces for aphids, scale insects, and thrips to eat.

48 When syrphid fly larvae seize their prey, they suck out the insides and then throw away the skin.

49 Ants that bite into the jewel caterpillar end up with sticky goo in their mouthparts. The goo comes from a coating on the caterpillar's warts.

50 The ambush bug has strong forelegs with teethlike structures that allow it to capture prey bigger than itself—including bumblebees.

51 Masked hunter nymphs cover themselves with dust and other debris. The disguise helps them ambush bedbugs, carpet beetles, and other prey.

52 African driver ants forage for food in large swarms. Using their large, scissor-like jaws, they can attack and devour other insects, birds, and snakes.

53 The Florida woods cockroach squirts an irritating fluid at its enemies. The fluid contains a mix of acids, alcohols, and other organic chemicals.

54 The cockroach releases the fluid with such force that the fluid can travel a distance of eight inches (20 cm).

55 An Amazon ant queen raids the nest of other ant species, driving out the adult ants and claiming the larvae as her own.

56 The ant queen uses a chemical scent to convince the larvae of the nest that she is their queen.

57 A tachinid fly may prey on a southern flannel moth larva as it is developing inside its cocoon.

58 The southern flannel moth caterpillar is covered in hairlike structures that give it a soft, furry appearance. The fur hides the caterpillar's dangerous spines.

59 In spite of its soft-looking appearance, the velvet ant has a tough exoskeleton that can be impossible for some predators to pierce.

60 MACLEAY'S SPECTRE—A TYPE OF STICK INSECT—RELEASES AN ODOR FROM ITS MOUTHPARTS WHEN DISTURBED.

61 The odor may smell foul to predators, but humans have compared it to the smell of toffee or peanut butter!

62 If the odor doesn't ward off predators, Macleay's spectre will use its thornlike spikes to defend itself.

63 The minute pirate bug is 0.1 inch (3 mm) long, but it can eat 30 spider mites in a day.

64 The feather-legged bug secretes a scent that ants find irresistible. As the ants move in, they become the bug's lunch.

65 The red spot assassin bug spits saliva when it's disturbed. The saliva can seriously harm and even digest an attacker.

66 The ant *Basiceros singularis* of Ecuador covers itself with mud so that it can remain hidden while stalking snails.

67 GROUND BEETLES WILL OFTEN RUN TO CATCH THEIR PREY, WHICH INCLUDES ANTS AND APHIDS.

68 The bush tiger mantis gets its name from its tigerlike habit of prowling the forest floor for prey.

69 Ichneumonid wasp larvae force the *Plesiometa argyra* spider to construct them a silk cocoon home. When the spider is finished, the larvae eat it.

70 Praying mantids have been known to kill and eat hummingbirds.

71 The beaded lacewing stuns its termite prey by "tooting" on it! The toot is a toxic vapor.

72 A jewel wasp drags a paralyzed cockroach into its lair and lays eggs in its abdomen. When the eggs hatch, the wasp larvae eat the cockroach.

73 To get much-needed protein, female adult maritime earwigs prey on eggs laid by members of their own species.

74 If the devil's flower mantis is startled while waiting to grab prey, it stands on its hind legs to look intimidating.

75 When burying beetle moms cannot provide enough food, they eat their own young.

1 IN A HONEYBEE COLONY, **WORKER BEES** ARE RESPONSIBLE FOR **FINDING FOOD,** WHICH IS MAINLY POLLEN AND NECTAR.

2 When a worker honeybee discovers a **FOOD SOURCE**, it returns to the hive to **INFORM OTHER MEMBERS** of its colony.

3 If a food source is less than 80 feet (24.4 m) from the hive, the bee performs a **CIRCULAR DANCE.** If the food source is farther away, it performs a **WAGGLE DANCE.**

4 To indicate that a food source is **ABUNDANT**, the worker honeybee will **CHANGE DIRECTION MANY TIMES** during its dance.

5 Honeybees store the pollen, which they use to make honey, in **POLLEN BASKETS.** These are rounded areas located on **EACH HIND LEG.**

6 An adult *Manduca sexta* moth will visit a **VARIETY OF FLOWERS,** but will drink nectar only from flowers that **EMIT A SMELL.**

25 WHOLESOME FACTS ABOUT INSECT

7 Adult moths and butterflies **SUCK UP NECTAR** through a long feeding tube called a **PROBOSCIS.**

8 **LOCUSTS** OFTEN SELECT WHICH PLANTS TO EAT BASED ON THE **NUTRIENTS** THEY CONTAIN.

9 Steel-blue sawfly larvae **FORAGE EUCALYPTUS LEAVES** in large groups, with one larva leading the way.

10 DUNG BEETLES USE THE GLOW OF THE **MILKY WAY** TO LIGHT THEIR WAY AS THEY ROLL THEIR FAVORITE TREAT: **DUNG.**

11 The beetles prefer the **SMELLIEST POOP,** which typically comes from animals that eat both **PLANTS** and **ANIMALS.**

12 Some stoneflies **LOSE THEIR MOUTHS** when they become adults and **DON'T EAT** at this stage in their life cycle.

13 The desert ant *Cataglyphis fortis* is a **SCAVENGER,** meaning it feeds on **DEAD ORGANISMS.**

14 To find food, *Cataglyphis fortis* relies on its **SENSE OF SMELL.** It can sniff out a **DEAD INSECT** up to 19.4 feet (5.9 m) away.

15 THE PAVEMENT ANT, AN INHABITANT OF **CITIES**, HAS AN APPETITE FOR HUMAN **JUNK FOOD**, WHICH IT FINDS CRUMBLED ON SIDEWALKS AND STREETS.

16 CLOTHES MOTH **LARVAE** feed on fabric made from animal fibers, such as WOOL, CASHMERE, and FUR.

17 Before some wasps **FORAGE FOR FOOD**, they fly several loops **AROUND THEIR NEST** to help identify its **LOCATION** and find their way back.

18 IT WAS ONCE BELIEVED THAT COCKROACHES FORAGE FOR FOOD **ALONE**, BUT IT IS NOW CLEAR THAT THEY **FOLLOW ONE ANOTHER** TO A FOOD SOURCE.

FORAGING

19 A DESERT LOCUST FEEDS ON **GREEN PLANTS** AND CAN EAT ITS BODY WEIGHT IN FOOD IN **JUST ONE DAY**.

20 Up to 80 MILLION desert locusts may gather in a large SWARM and descend on a farming area for a FEEDING FRENZY.

21 A LARGE SWARM OF DESERT LOCUSTS MAY EAT **423 MILLION POUNDS (192 MILLION KG)** OF PLANTS IN A DAY. THAT'S THE WEIGHT OF 12,800 LARGE SCHOOL BUSES.

22 TERMITE WORKERS CHEW UP WOOD AND LATER SECRETE THE DIGESTED MUSH TO THEIR COLONY MEMBERS TO FEED ON.

23 ANTS generally forage for food in groups. SCOUT ANTS find the food, and GATHERER ANTS bring it to the nest.

24

DRIVER ANT WORKERS, which eat other insects, have long, SHARP MANDIBLES that allow them to INFLICT PAIN on their victims.

25 THE ANT WORKERS USE THEIR LONG LEGS TO MOVE QUICKLY AND TO TRANSPORT PREY USUALLY SLUNG UNDERNEATH THEIR BODIES.

31

BUILDING FACTS ABOUT

1 Some caddisfly larvae build a protective case around themselves made of sticky silk, sand grains, and debris.

2 *Deuteragenia* wasps build nests with chambers for housing their larvae. Most of the chamber walls are made from plant material, resin, and soil.

3 The nest of the *Deuteragenia ossarium* wasp contains an outer chamber made of dead ants. The ant corpses may be used to ward off predators.

4 Adult weaver ants build leafy nests in treetops by weaving together leaves using silk produced by the larvae.

5 The mason bee constructs a bouquet-like nest on the ground. The nest is made of flower petals held together by mud.

6 For unknown reasons, mason bee nests vary by location. In Turkey, the bees select yellow, blue, pink, and purple petals. In Iran, only purple petals are used.

7 Termites use soil to create towering mounds that can reach 17 feet (5.2 m) high. The termites don't actually live inside the mound but beneath it.

8 Eastern tent caterpillars use strands of silk to create tentlike nests in trees. The tents shield them from the sun's heat and rain.

zebras by termite mound, Okonjima, Namibia, Africa

INSECT ARCHITECTS

9 Termite mounds may serve as air-conditioning units. They contain bubble-like chambers that allow air to flow through.

10 Adult *Trypoxylon politum*—an organ pipe mud dauber wasp—use mud and saliva to craft tubelike nests for their unhatched larvae.

11 Adult paper wasps chew up wood, leaves, and other materials to build papery, umbrella-shaped nests.

12 Meadow spittlebug nymphs live inside a frothy mass of "spit" they secrete.

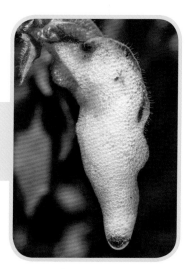

13 Leafcutter ant workers use their mandibles to dig connecting chambers and tunnels inside their nests.

14 The chambers serve different purposes. Some hold the leafcutter ants' fungus gardens, while others contain the colony's trash.

15 Yellow meadow ant colonies sometimes build mound nests if damp soil is available. They use plant roots and shoots to help hold the nests together.

15 FASCINATING FACTS ABOUT

Namib desert dune ant (*Camponotus detritus*) at entrance to nest

1 *Belgica antarctica* is a **midge that lives in Antarctica,** where winds can exceed **62 miles an hour (100 km/h).** The midge **lives in rock crevices and doesn't fly,** so it is not easily blown away.

2 Larvae of the **sleeping chironomid midge** of dry regions of Nigeria, Uganda, and Malawi may go for **eight months without water** in the dry season and still survive.

3 When the larvae lose most of their body water, they go into a dormant, or sleeplike, state until it eventually rains.

4 Larvae of the midge *Sergentia koschowi* have been discovered **4,462 feet (1,360 m)** beneath the surface of Lake Baikal in Russia. At this depth there is little to no oxygen.

5 The midge larvae probably have **hemoglobin—an oxygen-bearing protein—**in their bodies, helping them **survive.**

6 The Namib Desert dune ant lives in Africa's Namib Desert, where daytime temperatures can reach a scorching 140°F (60°C).

7 Namib Desert dune ants get their food and moisture by drinking honeydew from scale insects that live on plants.

INSECTS AT THE EXTREMES

8 The Namib Desert beetle is named after its African homeland, which gets very little rainfall each year. To stay hydrated, the beetle collects moisture from sea breezes.

9 The desert beetle leans into a sea breeze as it blows, allowing water droplets from the moist air to collect on its back.

10 *Cucujus clavipes*—an arctic beetle—has an antifreeze protein in its blood that allows the beetle to survive temperatures as low as minus 60°F (–51°C).

11 Bloodsucking arctic mosquitoes are serious pests in the summer months. On windless days, they form menacing swarms.

person in Alaska covered in mosquitos

12 Bumblebees have been discovered living 18,000 feet (5,486 m) above sea level on Mount Everest. At this altitude, the air is very thin.

13 To fly, bumblebees need to push their wings up against air to create lift—a difficult feat when the air is thin.

14 In 2014, NASA scientists sent a colony of 800 pavement ants to live aboard the International Space Station (ISS).

15 The low-gravity conditions aboard the ISS caused the ants to have trouble walking.

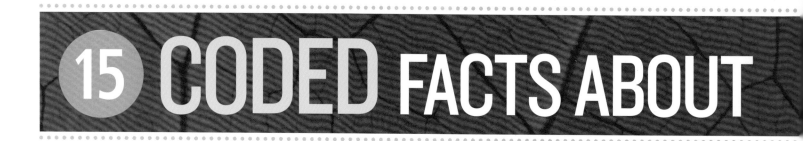

15 CODED FACTS ABOUT

❶ Insects, like all living things, have **genes**. Genes are units of **DNA**—the chemical code that **contains information** about an organism's characteristics.

❷ The midge *Belgica antarctica* has **13,500 genes**—the fewest known of any insect. Locusts have about 17,300—the most known. Humans have **24,000 genes.**

❸ **Millions of years ago,** wasp larvae attacked and infected **monarch butterfly caterpillars** with a virus. This virus **changed the genes** of the surviving caterpillars.

❹ As a result of the **wasp-inflicted virus,** monarch butterflies today have wasp genes that **protect them** against other viruses.

❺ Scientists have created an **insect family tree** using genetic information gathered from insect fossils. The family tree **spans more than 400 million years.**

❻ The family tree indicates that some **wasps, lacewings, beetles, flies,** and **crickets** living today resemble insect **ancestors** that lived alongside **dinosaurs.**

❼ **Blind water beetles** live in dark caves, so they don't have eyes. Yet these beetles have genes for **the sense of sight.**

INSECT GENES

8 Treehoppers sport unusual **helmets** that can resemble ants and thorns. The **genes** responsible for these helmets were once responsible for a **third set of wings** but were not activated.

9 Bedbugs seem to be able to **alter their genes** to become **resistant to pesticides** used against them.

10 Fruit flies can change about **5,000 of their genes** to adapt to **changes in temperature.**

11 The beetle mimic cockroach has "mom genes." A female can give birth to live young and provide them with nutrients from her own body.

12 A **virus** that infects gypsy moth caterpillars has a gene called egt that prevents them from **molting.**

13 The egt gene also prompts the caterpillars to **climb to treetops,** where they **die.**

14 The **queen and female workers** of a paper wasp colony **share a reproductive,** or egg-producing, **gene.**

15 The queen paper wasp's reproductive gene is active, or turned on, while the workers' reproductive gene is turned off.

diversity among butterfly pupae and adults produced by genes

1 Only FEMALE MOSQUITOES BITE HUMANS. Males feed on flower nectar. The females need the blood to PRODUCE EGGS.

2 A female mosquito has six MOUTHPARTS forming a TUBE: four are used to pierce and grip the host's skin and two to probe a CAPILLARY and channel BLOOD.

3 KISSING BUGS are named for their habit of biting humans around THEIR MOUTHS as they sleep.

4 FEMALE BLACK FLIES also need blood to produce EGGS. They will fly up to 10 MILES (16.1 KM) to find a blood meal.

5 Adult bedbugs are BROWN, but as they suck up their blood meal, they turn RED.

6 BEDBUGS hide during the day and COME OUT AT NIGHT to feed on the blood of humans. They also feed on PIGS and BATS.

25 PROBING FACTS ABOUT

7 THRIPS are tiny insects that PRICK PLANTS to feed on their SAP. Sometimes they prick PEOPLE instead but, getting no sap, they soon take off.

8 SCREWWORM FLY LARVAE can enter a human body through a cut in the skin. They DRILL DOWN TO THE BONE with their tusklike jaws.

9 HEAD LICE live among human hairs. Their mouths are lined with TINY HOOKS that LATCH ON THE SCALP as the louse draws blood.

10 SIX TO 12 MILLION PEOPLE in the United States get HEAD LICE each year.

11 Human itch mites BURROW into the upper layer of the skin, where they LAY THEIR EGGS. This often results in an ITCHY RASH.

12 Blacklegged tick nymphs suck the blood of people and large animals for three to four days. Then they drop to the forest floor and molt.

13 Sometimes, the nymphs suck and transmit blood infected with bacteria that cause LYME DISEASE.

14

In 1802, about 10,000 FRENCH TROOPS sent to the island of Hispaniola died from the disease YELLOW FEVER, which is transmitted by mosquitoes.

15 IN THE 1300s, **BUBONIC PLAGUE,** OR THE **BLACK DEATH,** KILLED MORE THAN 20 MILLION PEOPLE IN EUROPE. PLAGUE BACTERIA WERE SPREAD BY **RAT FLEAS** THAT BIT PEOPLE.

16 CHIGGER LARVAE, a type of mite, find a secluded area on human skin where they can hide. Then, they begin FEEDING ON HUMAN TISSUE.

17 **CHIGGERS,** like bedbugs and mosquitoes, can sense humans by the colorless and odorless gas they breathe out, called **CARBON DIOXIDE.**

INSECT STINGERS, BITERS, AND BLOODSUCKERS

18 *DEMODEX* MITES LIVE AT THE BASE OF HUMAN HAIR FOLLICLES, WHERE THEY FEED ON OIL AND BODY FLUIDS.

19 Despite their name, HORSE FLIES will feed on the blood of various livestock and humans. Females use their SCISSOR-LIKE MOUTHPARTS to cut through skin.

20 ALTHOUGH **CAT FLEAS** ARE ASSOCIATED WITH CATS, THEY CAN ALSO **FEED ON DOGS** AND OTHER ANIMALS— INCLUDING HUMANS.

21 Dog and cat fleas have in their hind legs a structure made of ELASTIC. This helps them JUMP up to 13 INCHES (33 CM) to escape their hosts' scratching legs.

22 **FIRE ANTS** don't normally feed on humans but, when threatened by them, will **PLUNGE THEIR VENOM-PACKED STINGERS** into skin.

23 Blowflies may lay their eggs in HUMAN CORPSES. After the larvae—or MAGGOTS— hatch, they eat their way through the body tissues.

24 Developed by entomologist Justin Schmidt, the **SCHMIDT PAIN INDEX RANKS 83 INSECT STINGS** on a scale of one to four, with four being the most painful.

25 The sting of the **TARANTULA HAWK,** a type of wasp, **GETS A FOUR ON** Schmidt's index. Schmidt describes the sting as "blinding, fierce, shockingly electric."

1 When **CRAZY ANTS** are stung by venom-packing fire ants, they secrete a substance that **NEUTRALIZES THE VENOM.**

2 When mice and other predators **CHOMP** on firefly larvae, they're left with a **TASTE** that's so **BITTER,** it keeps them from pursuing **FIREFLIES** in the future.

3 In case predators forget the taste, fireflies **FLASH THEIR LIGHTS** as a reminder. Predators will likely **RECALL** the lights from their previous encounter.

4 LARGE CABBAGE WHITE BUTTERFLY CATERPILLARS FEED ON CABBAGE LEAVES. WHEN THREATENED, THE CATERPILLARS *vomit their stinky meals* TO WARD OFF PREDATORS.

5 A BUTTERFLY'S WINGS are covered in scales. If the insect becomes entangled in a spider's web, its **SCALES DETACH,** allowing the butterfly to break free.

25 DARING FACTS ABOUT

7 OTHER MEMBERS IN THE TERMITE COLONY ARE **alerted to danger** BY A CHEMICAL IN THE FIRED GLUE. THIS PROMPTS THEM TO **begin shooting,** TOO.

8 One carpenter ant species in Malaysia has **POISON-PACKED GLANDS** that run from its jaws to its abdomen.

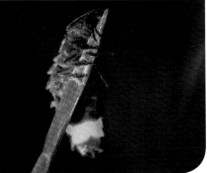

6 Nasutitermitine termites **FIRE A DEADLY GLUE** from their gunlike **SNOUTS.** The glue can travel several inches.

9 When this carpenter ant is attacked, it contracts its muscles, **CAUSING THE GLANDS TO EXPLODE.** This poison kills the predator—and the ant.

10 To confuse its predators, a **TRAP-JAW ANT** snaps its jaws shut with such force that it **CATAPULTS ITSELF** into the air.

11 Red-winged grasshoppers **STARTLE** their predators by **JUMPING** into the air, **FLASHING** their red hind wings, and making **CLACKING SOUNDS.**

12 Tiger moths **CONTAIN A TOXIN** that can harm or kill animals that **SNACK** on them.

13 To warn predatory bats of their toxin, TIGER MOTHS make CLICKING SOUNDS that bats can distinguish from other sounds.

14 When a *Heliothis* moth senses an approaching bat, IT FOLDS ITS WINGS close together and DROPS TO THE GROUND to avoid being detected.

15

A katydid RAISES ITS SPINE-COVERED LEGS in a menacing pose to scare its attackers.

16 Aphids PROVIDE ANTS WITH HONEYDEW, a sugary treat they secrete. In exchange for the honeydew, the ants PROTECT THE APHIDS from predators.

17 TO **STARTLE** LIZARDS AND OTHER PREDATORS, MALE ARMORED BUSH CRICKETS CREATE **LOUD, HARSH SOUNDS** BY RUBBING TOGETHER PARTS OF THEIR BODIES.

INSECT DEFENSES

18 IF THE SOUNDS DON'T STARTLE ATTACKERS, ARMORED BUSH CRICKETS SQUIRT BLOOD FROM THE SEAMS OF THEIR EXOSKELETONS.

19 Ironclad beetles **play dead** when they are threatened.

20 Flies have SPECIAL CELLS in their eyes that respond to CHANGES IN LIGHT. When an approaching predator casts a shadow, the flies make a quick getaway.

25 Clavate tortoise beetle larvae use their PREDATOR-REPELLANT POOP to make a PROTECTIVE SHIELD around themselves.

21 If attacked by a fish, the sunburst diving beetle EMITS STEROIDS THAT ARE TOXIC to the attacker.

22 Milkweed bugs SUCK UP TOXINS from whorled milkweed seeds. The toxins don't harm the bugs, but they are POISONOUS to the bugs' predators.

23 Milkweed bugs are black and BRIGHT REDDISH ORANGE. This bright tone acts as a WARNING COLOR, suggesting the insects are poisonous.

24 The bombardier beetle SPRAYS its attacker with BOILING CHEMICALS from a chamber located in its abdomen.

1
There are more than **20,000** bee species.

2
Honeybees and bumblebees are **social insects** that live together in large colonies, or nests, called **hives**.

3
A **hive** usually includes a **queen**, who lays eggs, and **female worker bees** that forage for food and take care of the queen and young.

4
Alongside the queen and female workers are **male drone bees**, which mate with the queen.

5
Up to **60,000 honeybees** can live together in a single hive.

6
Honeybee workers **secrete wax** and use it to make **six-sided cells** in the hive to store food, such as honey and plant nectar.

7
During **winter months**, nectar is scarce, so the bees survive by eating the **stored food**.

8
Megachile pluto is the **world's longest bee** species. Adult females can reach lengths of 1.5 inches (39 mm).

9
Megachile pluto bees **share their nests** with tree-dwelling **termites**.

10
About **90 percent** of all bee species are solitary—they live on their own. One such bee is the miner bee.

11
Female miner bees **dig nests in the ground.** They fill their nests with pollen and nectar to feed their young.

12
Eulaema quadragintanovem is a bee named for **Brazilian soccer player Ronaldinho Gaúcho.** *Quadragintanovem* is Latin for **49**—the number on Ronaldinho's jersey.

13
Bees are members of the order Hymenoptera, which means **"membrane"** and **"wings"** in Greek. The name refers to the members' **thin,** somewhat **transparent,** wings.

14
Bees **evolved from ancient wasps** more than 130 million years ago.

15
About 500 bee species are referred to as **stingless bees.** Their stingers are so small they cannot be used for defense.

16
Vulture bees don't eat nectar or pollen. Instead, they prefer **rotting flesh.**

17
Only **44 bee species** are known to **make honey.** They belong to the genus *Apis*.

18
Apis bees make honey from **flower nectar** by passing it from mouth to mouth until the moisture in it is reduced and it turns gooey.

19
The **flavor** of honey is determined by the source of the nectar. **Clover honey**—from the nectar of clover flowers—is one of the most popular.

20
In the 1950s, Brazilian scientists **bred bees from Africa** with local bees. The result was **Africanized honeybees**—also known as **killer bees.**

21
Africanized honeybees are **very aggressive.** The **slightest noise**—such as the sound of a lawn mower 100 feet (30.5 m) away—**can trigger them to attack.**

22
A bee's **buzzing** sound is usually made by the **beating of its wings.**

23
The wings of a bumblebee beat about **200 times a second.**

24
Up to **600 bumblebees** can live together in a **colony.** They inhabit **burrows** abandoned by birds, mice, or other bees.

25
A bumblebee queen creates **wax pots** inside the burrow. She **lays her eggs** inside these pots.

26
The queen also adds a mixture of pollen and nectar called **bee bread** to the wax pots as food for the **hatching larvae.**

27
Adult **carpenter bees** use their strong mandibles to **chew holes inside wood** to house their nests.

28
Carpenter bees prefer **softwoods,** such as **redwood, cedar, cypress,** and **pine.**

29
A female **leafcutter bee** may build her nest in **soil,** in a hollow **plant stalk,** or in a hollowed piece of **wood.**

50 Buzz-Worthy Facts About BEES

30 A female leafcutter bee uses her **mandibles** to cut **round pieces** from leaves. She **lines her nests** with these leafy bits.

34 *Anthophora pueblo*, a bee species found in **desert areas** of the southwestern United States, uses its mandibles to **drill nests in solid rock.**

38 Unlike the males of most bee species, which have yellow facial hair, the males of the **buff-tailed bumblebee** have **black hair** on their faces.

42 The blue-banded bee **bangs its head rapidly** against a tomato flower's stamens, where pollen is produced. This **causes the pollen to fall out** and spread.

46 African elephants are **afraid of bees.** These large animals run when they hear the buzzing sound of a **bee swarm.**

47 To help study **local bees,** scientists in New Hampshire, U.S.A., have built a "bee hotel" that houses about 250 bee species.

48 **Female cactus bees** use their heads to **jackhammer nesting holes** in the soil. They place their eggs in the holes along with nectar and pollen as food for the larvae.

31 *Perdita minima* is a species of **solitary bee** that builds its nests in **desert soil.**

32 An adult *Perdita minima* measures only .08 inch (2 mm) long. It's **so tiny** it can easily pass through the fine mesh of an insect net.

33 Sweat bees **drink human sweat and tears.** Salt and protein in these human fluids probably provide the bees with **nutrients.**

35 **Future generations** of *Anthophora pueblo* **reuse the nests** carved by their ancestors.

36 Bees can **process color three to four times** faster than humans. This ability probably helps the bees **locate flowers.**

37 Some honeybees in France are using **sugary waste** from candy factories to make honey. The **honey** matches the **blue** and **green** color of the candy.

39 Digger bees use their **mandibles** and **legs** to carve out nests in **desert soil.**

40 Like many insects, **bumblebees** can fly only when they are warm. To **heat up,** the bumblebees **shiver.**

41 By shivering, the bees **increase the temperature** of their thorax from **75.2°F (24°C) to 86°F (30°C)** in just a few seconds.

43 The burning feeling from a **bee sting** is caused by a **venom** called **melittin** that's released from the bee's stinger.

44 Orchid bees can fly up to **30 miles (48 km)** in a single trip.

45 To increase their **speed** while flying, orchid bees **swing their hind legs forward.**

49 A **swarm** of Japanese honeybees will attack a giant hornet by forming a ball around it. The bees' **vibrating muscles** then generate heat, **cooking** the hornet.

50 Inside the ball of Japanese honeybees it **can be as hot as 116°F (47°C).**

Honeybees store their honey, pollen, and larvae in hexagon-shaped cells.

1 Many prehistoric insects were PRESERVED in ANCIENT TREE SAP. The insects became stuck in the sap, which hardened into AMBER over time.

2 A piece of amber containing the EXOSKELETON of a stick insect nymph, a MUSHROOM, and a STRAND OF HAIR was discovered in 2016 in Russia.

3 The HAIR STRAND in the amber likely belonged to a SMALL MAMMAL that snipped the mushroom off a tree before the insect discovered it.

4 INSECT FOSSILS CAN ALSO BE FOUND IN LAYERS OF SEDIMENTARY ROCK, SUCH AS SHALE AND SANDSTONE.

5 This fossil of a large COCKROACH that lived millions of years ago shows that the insect had LONG LEGS and a MOVEABLE HEAD.

25 UNFORGETTABLE FACTS ABOUT

6 PLANT FOSSILS found in Patagonia, Argentina, have FEEDING MARKS made by ancient LEAF MINER LARVAE.

7 The WINGS OF A BEETLE that lived between 14 million and 20 million years ago were discovered in ANTARCTICA. Scientists believe the BEETLE lived in cold gravel near a stream.

8 The largest known insect to have lived is an ancient dragonfly-like insect, the griffinfly. Its wingspan was 27 inches (68.6 cm) from tip to tip.

9 A GRIFFINFLY FOSSIL was recently discovered in Kansas, U.S.A. The fossil, which was preserved in rock, is about 300 MILLION YEARS OLD.

10 The amount of OXYGEN IN THE AIR was much greater 300 million years ago than it is today. This made it possible for LARGE INSECTS to evolve.

11 SCIENTISTS RECENTLY FOUND A 100-YEAR-OLD FOSSIL OF A FRANKENSTEIN-LIKE INSECT. IT HAD A WASP'S FACE, AN ANT'S ANTENNAE, AND A COCKROACH'S BODY.

12 A 48-million-year-old SNAKE FOSSIL found in Germany had a LIZARD FOSSIL inside and, within this, were fossils of parts of INSECTS.

13 DRAGONFLIES the SIZE OF SEAGULLS roamed Earth about 300 million years ago.

14 CLAY CYLINDERS that were used as BEEHIVES about 3,000 YEARS ago have been found in ISRAEL.

15 The clay cylinders contained the REMAINS of ancient HONEYBEE workers, drones, pupae, and larvae.

18 Another amber fossil from Myanmar holds a LACEWING LARVA carrying DEBRIS such as sand grains and insect exoskeletons TO HIDE ITSELF.

16 A fossil discovered in Myanmar (Burma) shows a scale insect mom carrying 60 eggs on her back!

17 A piece of amber discovered in MYANMAR contains an individual of one ant species BATTLING with an ant of another species.

FORGOTTEN INSECTS

19 Fossils of **LEAFCUTTER BEE PUPAE** were excavated from the Rancho La Brea Tar Pits in California, U.S.A. The pupae were inside their **NEST CELLS.**

20 The leafcutter bee pupae lived between **23,000** and **40,000 YEARS AGO**— during the last **ICE AGE.**

21 A *Thanatophilus dispar* BEETLE that lived about 14,000 years ago was FOUND IN A BOG in Denmark.

24 The OLDEST INSECT FOSSIL ever found is 410 MILLION YEARS OLD. Scientists believe it was a flying insect.

22 By studying the beetle fossil and others like it, scientists determined that average WINTER TEMPERATURES at the time were about 1.3°F (−17°C).

23 A 46-MILLION-YEAR-OLD MOSQUITO fossil was discovered in layers of SHALE in Montana, U.S.A. The fossil is unusual because it shows the mosquito's FINAL BLOOD MEAL.

25 Studies of the fossil show that *Rhyniognatha hirsti* had SCISSOR-LIKE MOUTHPARTS, which it used to chew food.

1 Arachnids are invertebrates, or spineless animals, often mistaken for insects. The group includes spiders, scorpions, ticks, and mites.

2 Unlike insects, arachnids usually have four pairs of legs and a body with two segments—the abdomen and the cephalothorax, or a fused head and thorax.

3 More than 43,200 spider species have been discovered.

4 MANY SPIDERS HAVE EIGHT EYES—BUT THEY DON'T SEE VERY WELL. THEY USE THEIR EYES MAINLY TO DISTINGUISH BETWEEN LIGHT AND DARK.

5 Some spiders—like jumping spiders, flower spiders, and wolf spiders—have excellent vision. They use their eyesight to locate food.

6 Only 50 percent of all known spider species make webs to catch prey.

7 One acre (0.4 ha) of meadow may contain 2.25 million spiders. Each of these spiders will eat two insects a week for six months, which works out to about 117 million insects total.

8 The Himalayan jumping spider lives up to 21,980 feet (6,700 m) above sea level in the Himalayan Mountains in Asia.

9 Wolf spiders are named for their wolflike habit of chasing and pouncing on their prey.

10 The spider *Agelenopsis aperta* weaves funnel-shaped webs in tall desert grasses.

11 Jumping spiders can leap more than 20 times their body length in a single bound.

12 The Himalayan jumping spider often feeds on insects that have been blown up the mountain by wind.

13 One jumping spider—*Hasarius adansoni*—produces a dragline of silk as it jumps. This dragline keeps the spider steady and ensures a stable landing.

14 WEIGHT FOR WEIGHT, SPIDER SILK IS FIVE TO SIX TIMES STRONGER THAN A STEEL FIBER.

15 An *Agelenopsis aperta* weaves a web above its burrow. When an insect gets caught in the web, the spider scurries out to grab it and eat it.

16 In 2015, scientists discovered a peacock spider in Australia with bright blue and red stripes. They nicknamed it "Sparklemuffin."

17 Peacock spiders are known for the males' bright colors, which may be used to attract female mates.

18 Male peacock spiders also perform a dance to attract females. They raise a pair of legs and wave them around.

19 Spiders can have two, three, or four pairs of spinnerets, which are glands used to spin threads of silk.

20 The giant huntsman spider measures about 12 inches (30 cm) in diameter from leg tip to leg tip—bigger than a Frisbee.

21 Living up to its name, the giant huntsman hunts cockroaches and other prey by chasing or ambushing them.

22 In 2015, millions of spiders fell from the sky in Australia. Scientists believe the spiders were migrating and got swept up by strong winds.

23 THE SAMOAN MOSS IS THE SMALLEST OF SPIDERS. ITS BODY IS SMALLER THAN A PINHEAD.

24 To travel long distances, *Erigone* spiders release a strand of silk. A gust of wind picks up and blows the strand—and the spider. This behavior is called ballooning.

25 Spiders can travel hundreds of miles (km) by ballooning.

26 Linyphiid spiders can travel across water. They raise up their legs like sails and allow the wind to push them across the water's surface.

27 In the United Kingdom, linyphiid spiders are sometimes called money spiders.

28 Spiderweb designs include funnels, sheets, cobwebs—which are masses of tangled silk strands—and orbs, which are wheel-shaped.

29 SHEET WEBS ARE MADE OF SILK STRANDS THAT ARE NOT STICKY. PREY SIMPLY GET TANGLED IN THE STRANDS.

30 The happy-face spider relies on the happy-face pattern on its back to frighten predators.

31 The triangulate cobweb spider uses the bristles on its hind legs to wrap its victim in silk before getting close enough to bite it.

32 Many spiders, like cobweb weavers, make holes in their prey then vomit digestive fluids inside. The fluids break down the prey's soft parts so the spiders can suck them up.

33 The Australian golden orb spider weaves a strong, sticky, web that has a golden sheen in the sunlight.

34 This spider often wraps its captured prey in silk and stores it above its web to eat when food is scarce.

35 A female wolf spider lays several dozen eggs, which she wraps together in a silk sac and carries on her back.

36 After the wolf spider eggs hatch, the tiny spiderlings climb onto their mother's back. She continues to carry them for several days.

During summers, millions of spiders may live in an area of meadow like this.

75 COOL FACTS ABOUT

37 If hungry, the female black widow spider will often kill and eat a male black widow after mating.

38 The Brazilian wandering spider is the deadliest spider in the world. Its venom is poisonous to humans, attacking the nervous system.

39 Tarantulas may create a trip wire with their silk. When an insect triggers the wire, the spider scurries out of its burrow and uses its legs to grab its victim.

40 TARANTULAS ALSO FEED ON FROGS, MICE, AND SMALL LIZARDS.

41 The *Cyclosa* spider of Peru is less than .25 inch (0.6 cm) long, which can make it easy prey for large predators.

42 To defend itself against predators such as tarantula hawks, a Chilean rose tarantula will flick its irritating hairs at the attacker.

43 To scare predators away, the *Cyclosa* spider uses leaves, debris, and insect corpses to craft a decoy. The decoy looks like a larger version of itself.

44 Critters in the order Opilones—often called daddy longlegs or harvestmen—are not spiders. Unlike spiders, they have two eyes and do not produce silk or venom.

45 Scorpions glow in the moonlight. Some scientists believe this helps scorpions recognize each other or confuse their prey.

46 ALMOST 2,000 SCORPION SPECIES HAVE BEEN DISCOVERED.

47 The rock scorpion, which lives in South Africa, is the world's longest scorpion. Females can grow up to 8.3 inches (21 cm) in length.

48 The Caribbean-dwelling *Microtityus fundorai* is the smallest scorpion. Adults reach only 0.5 inch (13 mm) in length.

49 Camel spiders are arachnids that can reach 6 inches (15 cm) in length. They look a little like spiders and a little like scorpions but they are neither.

50 Before mating, a male scorpion grasps the female with his pincers. Then they perform a dance known as the *promenade à deux*—French for "walking together."

51 The scorpions' mating dance consists of sideways and backward movements. The dance can go on for an hour.

52 Instead of laying eggs, scorpions give birth to live young.

53 Mites of the order Mesostigmata feed on the blood of animals—including humans.

54 After scorpions are born, they crawl onto their mother's back, where they can remain for up to 50 days.

55 Scorpions are born white and have a soft outer covering.

56 Young scorpions molt, or shed their outer covering, several times before becoming adults.

57 Camel spiders are fast runners. They can reach speeds of 10 miles an hour (16 km/h).

58 To eat their prey, many scorpions secrete digestive fluids from their midgut area. The fluids break down the soft parts of the prey, which the scorpion then sucks up.

59 Scorpions have venom-producing stingers in their tails. They use the stingers against predators or to paralyze struggling prey.

60 Meerkats, which eat scorpions, will disarm the arachnids by breaking off their tails. They teach their pups to do the same.

61 THE SOUTH AFRICAN FAT-TAIL SCORPION CAN SQUIRT VENOM AT ITS PREDATORS.

62 The two-spotted spider mite uses its needlelike mouthparts to puncture leaves and suck up the plant sap.

63 Camel spiders belong to an order called Solifugae, which means "those who flee from the sun." They prefer shade to the sun's hot rays.

64 Some scorpion burrows have a platform that can be used as a front porch, and a chamber where the scorpion rests and feeds.

65 A spiral tunnel links the porch and the chamber. Navigating the tunnel is usually too difficult for the scorpions' predators.

66 In 2013, scientists found a new scorpion species in Turkey. *Euscorpius lycius* is named after Lycia, an ancient region in present-day Turkey.

67 Dust mites can often be found in people's homes, where the air is warm and humid.

68 Tail-less whip scorpions aren't scorpions. They are arachnids known for their long, whiplike front legs, which they use as feelers.

69 MORE THAN 48,000 MITE SPECIES HAVE BEEN DISCOVERED.

70 The venom of the Indian red scorpion is one of the deadliest. In humans it can cause nausea, breathing problems, and heart attacks.

71 All scorpions are nocturnal, hunting and feeding at night.

72 The emperor scorpion has fine hairs on its pincers and tail that can detect air and ground vibrations made by its prey.

73 Dust mites feed on dead skin, and are a cause of dust-related allergies.

74 About 900 tick species have been discovered. All species feed on blood.

75 American dog ticks can feed on the blood of their host for several days.

INSECT COUSINS

1 If a wasp threatens the young of a female **THORN BUG,** she will give the predator a **POWERFUL KICK** with her club-shaped hind legs.

2 The hibiscus harlequin beetle **SHEPHERDS HER NYMPHS** across plants as they feed. She leaves them only when they are **MATURE ENOUGH** to care for themselves.

3 When hungry, some burying beetle larvae **STROKE** their parents' mandibles. Mom and dad then eat a **DEAD ANIMAL'S FLESH** and vomit into the larvae's mouths.

4 For their species to survive, some insects **LAY LOTS OF EGGS.** For example, the African driver ant queen lays up to **FOUR MILLION** eggs every 25 days.

5 The female **GHOST MOTH** has no relationship with her young. In mid-flight, she **DROPS HER EGGS** in random locations and flies away.

6 White-margined burrowing bug nymphs mature in the **SOIL** as their moms stand guard and feed them **MINT SEEDS.**

25 CARING FACTS ABOUT

7 A sycamore lace bug mom **SCATTERS HER EGGS** across many leaves to **REDUCE THE RISK** of predators eating all her eggs.

8 DEAD LEAF PRAYING MANTIS FEMALES **STAND GUARD** OVER THEIR HIDDEN EGG SACS, **READY TO ATTACK** ANY PREDATOR THAT ATTEMPTS TO GRAB THEM.

9 *Aetalion reticulatum* **TREEHOPPER** females watch their eggs until they hatch. Then, **ANTS** look after the young in exchange for the nymphs' **HONEYDEW.**

10 Wood roach nymphs aren't able to **digest wood,** which is essential to their diet. So their parents **feed them fluids** from their rear ends.

11 To protect her **YOUNG NYMPHS** from a damselfly, a female *Gargaphia* bug **JUMPS ON THE PREDATOR'S BACK** while her nymphs make their getaway.

12 Korean wood-feeding cockroach nymphs grow much faster **if raised by** two parents instead of one.

13 A pair of *Nicrophorus* **CARRION BEETLES** will strip the skin of a dead animal, mold its flesh into a ball, and **LAY THEIR EGGS INSIDE.**

14 FEMALE *LETHOCERUS* WATER BUGS LAY EGGS ON A **stick** ABOVE THE WATER. TO KEEP THE EGGS **moist,** THE MALES SPRINKLE **droplets of water** ON THEM.

15 A female *Belostoma* water bug GLUES HER EGGS to a MALE BUG'S BACK.

16 Brazilian tortoise beetle larvae **CROWD UNDERNEATH** and around their mother's body for **PROTECTION.**

17 Female Japanese burrowing bugs **CARE FOR THEIR YOUNG** on the **FALLEN FRUITS** of *Schoepfia* trees. The bugs mate only when the fruits are **IN SEASON.**

INSECT FAMILIES

18 ANTS THRIVE IN **warm, humid** CONDITIONS. ADULT ANTS WILL CONSTANTLY MOVE THEIR **eggs** AND **larvae** WITHIN THE NEST TO GIVE THEM THE BEST **living conditions.**

19 Some shield bug moms produce a **FOUL-SMELLING** secretion that deters predators from her **NYMPHS.**

25 AN EGGPLANT LACE BUG FEMALE WILL HOLD OFF LAYING EGGS UNTIL HER EXISTING NYMPHS HAVE MATURED INTO ADULTS.

20 Males and females of some *Cephalodesmius* dung beetles **WORK TOGETHER** to provide their larvae with a **STINKY MEAL** of leaves, flowers, fruits, and poop.

21 SALT-MARSH BEETLE MOMS LAY THEIR EGGS IN BOTTLE-SHAPED CHAMBERS THEY DIG ALONG SANDY SHORELINES.

22 When the tide comes in, the moms **BLOCK THE CHAMBER OPENINGS** with their bodies to prevent water from getting in and drowning the eggs.

23 When there isn't enough food for BURYING BEETLE LARVAE to eat, their parents EAT some of them to reduce the MOUTHS they have to feed.

24 Some **LEAF BEETLE** and **COCKROACH** females don't lay eggs. Instead, they nourish their young inside their bodies and **GIVE BIRTH TO LIVE YOUNG.**

49

❶ When a bumblebee lands on a flower, pollen grains get caught in its hair. The grains are transferred to the next flower the bee visits.

❷ About 80 percent of all flowering plants are pollinated by animals, with insects being the major contributors.

❸ A single southeastern blueberry bee pollinates enough of those flowers to produce more than 6,000 blueberries.

❹ Female mosquitoes drink mostly blood, but all mosquitoes feed on nectar—and some, like snowpool mosquitoes, pollinate flowers in the process.

❺ As a snowpool mosquito laps nectar from a blunt-leaf orchid, pollen sticks to its eyes. The pollen is deposited on a special receptor of the next orchid.

❻ A female yucca moth scrapes pollen from a flower, shapes it into a lump, and carries it to another flower, where she deposits it.

❼ Alkali bees are pollinators of alfalfa—a nutritious plant that's often used to feed livestock.

❽ For years, U.S. alfalfa farmers thought the bees were pests and used pesticides to kill them. As their alfalfa yields decreased, they realized the bees' importance.

INSECT HELPERS

a bee pollinating a flower as it collects pollen

9 The giant Amazon water lily attracts beetles with its scent and radiating warmth. As the beetles enter, the flower closes, dusting them with pollen.

10 The corpse flower smells like rotting meat, so it attracts pollinators like flesh flies, which feed on dead flesh.

11 Flesh flies examine the smelly corpse flower for meat, but they never find it. As they search, they distribute the flower's pollen.

12 Male *Euglossa* bees are drawn to bucket orchids for their oils, which they use to attract female mates. As the male bees collect the oils—they pollinate the flowers.

13 Some insects, like the *Cotesia congregata* wasp, aren't involved in pollination, but they help plants by killing pests that feed on them.

14 The female wasp injects her eggs into a tomato hornworm, which feeds on tomato plants. When the eggs hatch, the larvae feed on the hornworm.

15 In Spain, ladybugs are a good indicator of an olive orchard's health. The more ladybugs present, the healthier the orchard.

❶ Each fall, millions of **monarch butterflies** leave Canada and head to **Mexico** to lay their eggs.

❷ **Mormon crickets** travel more than 50 miles (80.5 km) **to find food** and to **escape being eaten** by their own species.

❸ Some **migrating** moths travel at heights where **wind currents** are fastest, helping them reach their destination quicker.

❹ When **Florida harvest ant** colonies move to a new location, they mark their territory by forming a **circle of debris** around the new nest.

❺ Before setting off, **worker giant tropical honeybees** perform a **migration dance** to tell the colony in which direction to travel.

❻ A horse fly larva lives on **moist cow dung** until it matures. At that point it migrates to **dry cow dung**, where it pupates.

❼ **Wingless female aphids** migrate from their host trees to **leafy plants**, where they produce many **generations** of aphids.

❽ The **globe skimmer** travels up to **18,000 miles** (28,968 km) to lay its eggs.

INSECT MIGRATION

9 The larvae of the valley black gnat live in the pores of **wet clay** and **adobe-rich soils**. After they mature, they migrate to the **surface**.

10 Scientists **tracked the migration** of honeybees by sticking a **tiny radar antenna** to each insect's body and following its movement using a **mobile tracking station**.

11 To **escape warming temperatures** in foothills of Mount Kinabalu in **Borneo**, Geometridae moths move 220 feet (67 m) uphill, to where the climate is cooler.

12 Warming temperatures have also forced the **comma butterfly** to move 137 **miles (220 km) north** from central England to Edinburgh, Scotland.

13 The **painted-lady butterflies** that return home to East Africa from their migration to the Arctic Circle are the **great-great-great-great grandkids** of the butterflies that started the trip.

14 During the fall, when their **food supply decreases**, convergent ladybugs gather together in groups and **move from grasslands** to **mountain regions**.

a laboratory study of the flight of a desert locust

15 When there isn't much **vegetation** to feed on, **desert locusts swarm** to a new area where crops are **plentiful**. This also keeps them from eating one another.

1 SILK fabrics, made from the silk spun by *Bombyx mori* moth larvae, have been part of CHINESE CULTURE for more than 4,500 years.

2 During the Mughal era in INDIA (1526–1857), many FINE GARMENTS worn by royalty were decorated with small bits of BEETLE FOREWINGS.

3 High-ranking members of the NAGA TRIBES in northeast India wear garments DECORATED with beetle wings as a symbol of their own IMPORTANCE.

4 During China's Tang dynasty (A.D. 618–907), people kept CRICKETS in GOLDEN CAGES. At night, they enjoyed the crickets' CHIRPING SONGS.

5 Some **American Indian** groups once used cocoons of saturniid moths to make **hand** and **ankle rattles**, and **necklaces**.

25 FASHIONABLE FACTS ABOUT

6 Napoleon I of France had HONEYBEE IMAGES displayed throughout his ROYAL PALACE.

7 People in Brazil once used FIREFLIES IN LANTERNS, which they attached to their ANKLES to light their way in the dark.

8 FLEA CIRCUSES were popular in ENGLAND and GERMANY during the 1800s and 1900s. They featured fleas performing acts such as pulling miniature carts.

10 MORE THAN 300 ANCIENT GREEK COINS WITH PICTURES OF INSECTS AND ARACHNIDS HAVE BEEN DISCOVERED.

9 ANCIENT EGYPTIANS wore AMULETS—a type of jewelry—that were shaped like SCARAB BEETLES and believed to bring the wearers PROTECTION and a long life.

11 The MAYA PEOPLE, who once lived in present-day Central America, dyed their fabrics with a RED POWDER made from COCHINEAL SCALE INSECTS.

12 Some historians believe that ancient Egyptian ruler CLEOPATRA may have used LIPSTICK made from kermes oak SCALE INSECTS.

WILLIAM FOX PRESENTS
Theda Bara
CLEOPATRA

13 AN AZTEC WARRIOR WHO CAPTURED AN ENEMY IN BATTLE WAS AWARDED A BLACK ORNAMENT SHAPED LIKE A BUTTERFLY.

14 AMULETS shaped like CICADAS were once placed on the tongues of the dead in CHINA in the belief it would help them move on to the AFTERLIFE.

15 HOPI INDIANS believe that their ancestors have taken the form of insects such as WASPS, BEES, and CICADAS. So, to honor them, they make figures wearing insect masks.

16 Wasps have a NARROW JUNCTION between their thorax and abdomen. This "WASP WAIST" inspired a woman's corset in the 1800s.

17 The "BEEHIVE" was a popular HAIRSTYLE in the mid-1960s. It wasn't inspired by a beehive but by the front of B-52 AIRCRAFT used during World War II.

INSECT FADS

18 In Peru, men of the AGUARUNA TRIBE make hanging EARRINGS from seeds, toucan feathers, and BEETLE WINGS.

19 In 2010, British fashion designer ALEXANDER McQUEEN created a line of clothes inspired by the PATTERNS OF INSECTS such as moths and butterflies.

20 CADDISFLY LARVAE, which are known for making silk and constructing shelters from DEBRIS, are being used by JEWELRY vendors to create unique jewelry.

21 Instead of debris, the vendors give the caddisfly larvae little gemstones. The larvae then make sparkly shelters, which are sold as jewelry.

22 GOLD FLY PENDANTS were found in the temple of Queen Ahhotep, an ancient Egyptian ruler who lived more than 6,500 years ago.

23 During the Victorian era, from 1837 to 1901, people used the wings of MADAGASCAN SUNSET MOTHS to make JEWELRY.

24 MULTICOLORED BUTTERFLY WINGS have been used to DECORATE paintings, trays, and paperweights. This tradition has ceased—to protect and conserve butterflies.

25 In the 1980s, many American children snuggled with plush toys called GLO WORMS. A gentle squeeze would cause the toys to glow.

1 A water strider male TAPS THE WATER'S SURFACE with his legs until the female is READY TO MATE.

2 A female praying mantid often kills her partner once he has FERTILIZED HER EGGS.

3 The MORE SPIT that male scorpion flies secrete, the better their chances of ATTRACTING MATES.

4 SOAPBERRY BUGS can mate for up to 11 DAYS.

5 Male and female fireflies use their FLASHING LIGHTS to communicate with each other while COURTING.

11 Female queen butterflies FLAP THEIR WINGS to attract a male's attention.

12 Female mosquitoes attract a male's attention with a HUMMING SOUND they make by VIBRATING THEIR WINGS.

13 A male silk moth may detect a female's CHEMICAL SCENTS from more than ONE MILE (1.6 km) away.

14 The king and queen of a termite colony MATE FOR LIFE.

15 Male giraffe weevils BATTLE EACH OTHER with their necks for the right to mate with a female.

A pair of common blue butterflies share a flower.

35 LOVELY FACTS ABOUT

6 Male mayflies may SIT ON TOP of a YOUNG FEMALE, waiting until she is MATURE ENOUGH to mate.

7 Male honeybee DRONES will mate with the queen IN MID-FLIGHT.

8 The male balloon fly spins a SILK BALLOON, which he presents as a GIFT to his female partner.

9 Some MALE BALLOON FLIES also bring the female a DEAD INSECT to feed on while mating.

10 Female hangingflies choose their mates based on their ABILITY TO CATCH PREY.

16 Male bush crickets CALL OUT to females with CHIRPING SOUNDS made by rubbing together two parts of their bodies.

17 The male mole cricket's MEGAPHONE-SHAPED BURROW amplifies his chirping—it can be heard up to 2,000 feet (610 m) away.

18 When FIELD CRICKETS are attacked, the male lets his female companion RUN INTO THE BURROW before he does.

19 Springtails tease each other during courtship. The female will PRETEND TO RUN AWAY while the male tries to catch her.

20 Potato aphids are LESS LIKELY TO COURT and mate when they DETECT STORMS.

21 A male GIANT WATER BUG will do PUSH-UPS in the water to attract females.

22 Male bow-winged grasshoppers near BUSY ROADS produce more high-pitched MATING CHIRPS than average, to be heard above traffic.

23 A male thorn bug calls out to a female by VIBRATING HIS ABDOMEN. If interested, the female RETURNS THE CALL.

24 Male paper wasps come together in COMMON AREAS CALLED LEKS, where a female wasp will choose one male to be her mate.

25 Female paper wasps usually choose the male with the largest abdominal YELLOW SPOTS and the BLACKEST head.

26 Tropical house cricket females MARK THEIR MATES with a SCENT so that they avoid mating with them again.

27 Dung beetle males and females MEET each other at their POOP-FILLED feeding sites.

28 Before mating, the male fruit fly TAPS the female with his leg. The two flies then PERFORM A DANCE.

29 Male smoke flies form SWARMS in the smoke of FIRE. A female enters the swarm to be COURTED.

30 After a male queen butterfly catches his female mate, he RUBS HIS SCENT on her ANTENNAE.

31 LOVEBUG COUPLES can be seen FLYING WHILE ATTACHED to each other.

32 Male skippers have special WING SCALES that produce a SCENT that attracts female skippers for mating.

33 A jewelwing dragonfly male may try to SEPARATE a rival male from a female by BUMPING INTO the couple.

34 A red-horned robber fly male PERFORMS A DANCE for the female that involves BOBBING HIS ABDOMEN up and down.

35 Eastern dobsonfly males use their SICKLE-SHAPED JAWS to BATTLE RIVALS for a chance to mate with a female.

LOVE BUGS

15 HIGH-TECH FACTS ABOUT

① Some **female wood wasps** use **needlelike organs** to gently bore into trees. A **surgical robot**, inspired by the wasps, bores into **human brains** in the same delicate manner.

② A new **sensor technology** that may **prevent car crashes** was inspired by locusts' ability to **avoid collisions while flying**.

③ Space aeronautical engineers have developed small **flying robots** that may be used to **explore Mars**. The robots generate most of their **lift**—an upward force—by **flapping mechanical wings** in the same way that insects flap their wings.

an artist's impression of a flying insect robot exploring Mars

④ Engineers studied insect **exoskeletons** to create "shrilk," an **environmentally safe material** they hope will one day replace non-biodegradable plastic.

⑤ Some **TV** companies have introduced **reflection-free screens**. The screens are modeled after **moth eyes**, which have special patterns that prevent light from reflecting off them.

⑥ **Diving beetles** have tiny hairs that work underwater like **suction cups**. Scientists are studying these hairs to create better underwater devices for **scuba divers**.

⑦ Scientists looked to aquatic insects for inspiration while developing **water-rescue robots**. The robots can move across the surface of ponds like **water striders**, and can jump like **fleas**.

⑧ Scientists have built **ant robots** that leave **light trails** for their fellow robots to follow.

INSECT-INSPIRED MACHINES

9 Flies are able to detect movements in shadows and see moving objects against busy backgrounds. These motion-detecting abilities are now inspiring better video cameras.

10 Diving beetles trap air underwater to breathe. By studying this ability, scientists hope to create artificial gills that could help divers operate underwater.

11 To develop better hearing aids, scientists are studying the *Ormia ochracea* fly, which relies on its supersensitive hearing abilities to detect crickets.

12 Fog beetles have ridges on their backs to collect water droplets from fog. A new water bottle with ridges does the same, and may help people access clean water in areas experiencing a water shortage.

13 Scales on butterfly wings reflect light. This allows us to see their bright colors. Some e-reader screens, inspired by butterflies, display color in this manner.

14 Termites keep air flowing through their mounds by opening and closing vents. Some architects are now designing cooling systems for buildings based on these vented structures in nature.

15 Army ants form large swarms to defend themselves against intruders. Scientists studied this behavior to develop software that protects computers from viruses.

15 MOUTHWATERING FACTS ABOUT

❶ More than two billion people around the world regularly eat insects. The critters are especially popular in parts of Central Africa and Southeast Asia.

❷ 1,900 insect species are safe to eat.

❸ Beetles are the most popular insects to eat. It is their larval stage—mealworms and grubs, for example—that is usually eaten.

❹ The most commonly eaten beetles include the long-horned, June, dung, and rhinoceros beetles.

❺ After eating shrimp for the first time, the Goshute Indians in western Utah, U.S.A., called them sea crickets because they reminded them of the crickets they ate.

❻ Edible emperor moth caterpillars—often called mopani worms—contain three times the amount of protein as beef.

❼ In some markets in Uganda, Africa, edible grasshoppers are more expensive than beef.

❽ One restaurant in Wales serves a bug burger made with toasted crickets, mealworms, grasshoppers, spinach, and sun-dried tomatoes.

APPETIZING INSECTS

deep-fried beetles, mealworms, crickets—and various arachnids—on sale to eat in Guangzhou, China

9 The practice of eating insects is called entomophagy. The word comes from the Greek terms *éntomon*, which means "insect," and *phagein*, meaning "to eat."

10 In the Democratic Republic of the Congo in Africa, some tribes stew termites and use the leftover fat to cook meat.

11 Chinese scientists created a silkworm cookie for astronauts to eat in space as a source of protein.

12 A 3.5-ounce (99-g) portion of peanut butter may contain 30 insect parts. Health experts believe this is safe to eat.

13 You can order grasshopper guacamole in one restaurant in Colorado, U.S.A.

14 Cossid moth larvae were often eaten by Aboriginals in Australia, where they are known as witchetty grubs.

15 Stink bugs add an apple flavor to sauces.

❶ Social insects—such as ants, termites, and some bees and wasps—live together with other members of their species.

❷ All insect societies include many generations that work together to care for their colony's young.

❸ In the *Bombus huntii* bee colony, some bees shiver to create warmth for the nest. The higher temperature helps the larvae develop inside their eggs.

❹ If the temperature of the nest is too high, another group of bees in the colony fan their wings to cool things off.

❺ When holes appear in the walls of their woody homes, social aphids rely on their soldiers to repair them. The soldiers use body fluids to plug the holes.

❻ Termites often bury dead members of their colony in distant parts of the nest.

❼ When a common red ant dies, its decaying corpse can be a health risk to the colony. So, worker ants will move its body away from the nest.

❽ Social wasp colonies are started in the spring by a queen, who builds a nest and lays eggs.

INSECT SOCIETIES

9 The wasp colony can grow to 5,000 members. By winter, all members die except for a queen, who begins a new colony the following spring.

10 A termite queen's children are her workers. They clean her and care for the eggs she lays.

11 Termite queens lay an egg every three seconds. Throughout their 15-year life span, each queen can lay more than a quarter-billion eggs.

12 A black garden ant colony usually has several queens. But the workers gradually kill them off until only one remains.

13 To ensure that queen bees can reproduce, worker honeybees feed them royal jelly—a substance made of water, proteins, and sugar.

14 A northern paper wasp can recognize and remember the faces of its colony members.

15 Eastern tent moth caterpillars live with their siblings in silk tents woven on tree branches. Up to 200 caterpillars can share a tent.

queen termites and attendant workers

1 The national insect of Latvia is the two-spotted ladybug.

2 The Entomology Museum, an insect museum in Yangling, China, is shaped like a ladybug.

the giant bee at the Eden Project, England

3 Each November, about 1,000 people gather in Kushihara, Japan, to eat wasp larvae at the Hebo Festival.

4 The University of Arkansas at Monticello, U.S.A., named its football team the Boll Weevils. The school chose the insect as representative of the team's toughness.

5 A giant bee sculpture sits in the garden of the Eden Project in Cornwall, England. The sculpture is made from recycled scrap.

6 The European praying mantis is the state insect of Connecticut, U.S.A.

7 Legend has it that Isabella tiger moth caterpillars—known as woolly worms—can be used to predict the weather, inspiring the annual Woolly Worm Festival in Kentucky, U.S.A.

FACTS ABOUT INSECTS

8 In Kamakura, Japan, you can visit a monument that honors insects killed by humans. The monument features a woman holding a beetle-like creature.

9 The Fire Ant Festival takes place each October in Marshall, Texas, U.S.A. During the ant-themed event, several artists create giant fire ant sculptures.

10 *Musca*, which means "fly" in Latin, is a constellation, or star pattern, that can be seen from countries south of the Equator.

11 In 2010, artists created sand sculptures shaped like insects and arachnids at the Creepy Crawlies Exhibition in Melbourne, Australia.

12 The monarch butterfly is the U.S. state insect of Alabama, Idaho, Illinois, Minnesota, Texas, Vermont, and West Virginia.

13 In an outdoor sculpture called Queen Bee in Melbourne, Australia, a giant model of a queen bee sits atop a structure with worker bees below.

14 The Butterfly Parade and Bazaar takes place each October in Monterey, California, U.S.A. The event celebrates western monarch butterflies' returning to their winter grounds.

15 Pestival is an insect festival established in the United Kingdom. It is a mix of art, science, and music—with a message to "respect every insect."

1 Australian meat ants USE THEIR ANTENNAE to send and receive chemical signals.

2 When their colony is disturbed, termite soldiers create WARNING MESSAGES by BANGING THEIR HEADS against colony surfaces.

3 When other termites in the colony DETECT VIBRATIONS made by the soldiers' banging, they know something is wrong.

4 The FIREFLY COMMUNICATOR gadget attracts fireflies by EMITTING LIGHT SIGNALS they can recognize.

5 Each firefly species has a UNIQUE FLASHING PATTERN. Members of a species use the pattern to RECOGNIZE one another.

11 Synchronous fireflies flash their five to eight yellow lights AT THE SAME TIME.

12 As one golden-backed ant follows another, it TOUCHES THE LEADER to indicate it is one step behind.

13 If the golden-backed ant leader does not feel its follower, it will STOP AND TURN AROUND.

14 If threatened, mature pupae of the ant *Myrmica scabrinodis* MAKE SOUNDS to call for worker ants to protect them.

19 Male ghost fireflies communicate with females by GLOWING with a BLUE or GREEN LIGHT.

20 Male katydids of the same species have a UNIQUE CHIRPING SONG they use to call out to females.

21 The common true katydid male produces a chirping song that SOUNDS LIKE the insect is saying "KATY-DID, KATY-DIDN'T."

26 Carpenter ants can EXCHANGE MESSAGES by releasing BEHAVIOR-ALTERING substances into each other's mouths.

27 A common whitetail dragonfly tells another dragonfly to BUZZ OFF by raising its abdomen.

28 Madagascar hissing cockroach males HISS AT RIVALS during BATTLES for supremacy.

32 Ponerine army ant workers tell their colony members it's TIME TO MOVE by producing CLICKING SOUNDS with their mandibles.

33 German cockroaches use CHEMICAL MESSAGES to communicate with each other about the LOCATION OF FOOD.

34 Oriental hornet larvae SIGNAL THEY ARE HUNGRY by scraping their mandibles against the walls of their cells.

35 The QUEEN of a *Myrmica schencki* ant colony MAKES RUBBING SOUNDS to remind the workers she's the boss.

35 WIRED-UP FACTS ABOUT

6
Root-eating cabbage flies DETER LEAF-EATING INSECTS from devouring their mustard plants by producing a NOXIOUS CHEMICAL.

7
Masked birch caterpillars RUB THE HAIRS ON THEIR REARS against leaves to make vibrations. This keeps intruders away.

8
A masked birch caterpillar uses different vibrations to CONTACT FELLOW CATERPILLARS to help build a shelter.

9
A honeybee performs a WAGGLE DANCE—a shimmy in a figure-eight pattern—to give its hive members the location of a food source.

10
If the food is in a DANGEROUS AREA, honeybees will MAKE BEEP SOUNDS with their flight muscles to warn other bees to be careful.

15
Asian and European honeybees that share a hive can LEARN EACH OTHER'S DANCE LANGUAGES.

16
If separated from its group, a spitfire sawfly larva sends a DISTRESS CALL by TAPPING a leaf surface.

17
When the other spitfire sawfly larvae detect the LOST MEMBER'S CALL, they tap back to CONVEY THEIR LOCATION.

18
Calloconophora pinguis treehoppers SIGNAL to others that a leaf food source is DAMAGED by moving their legs as if running in place.

22
Blue-and-white longwing butterflies make CLICKING SOUNDS to SHOO RIVALS out of their territory.

23
Monarch butterflies OPEN AND CLOSE THEIR WINGS while roosting to keep other monarchs from landing on them.

24
Female monarch butterflies emit a CHEMICAL SCENT called a pheromone to get a male monarch's ATTENTION.

25
Argentine ant scouts create a CHEMICAL TRAIL that LEADS THEIR COLONY MEMBERS to a food source.

29
Deathwatch beetle males call out to mates with TICKING sounds. They produce the sounds by BANGING THEIR HEADS against trees.

30
A bess beetle can produce 14 DIFFERENT SOUNDS by rubbing its hind wings against its abdomen.

31
When male FRUIT FLIES approach a mate they produce a SONG by extending and FANNING one of their wings.

Fireflies light up the night.

INSECT COMMUNICATION

15 BOLD FACTS ABOUT INSECT

1 Insect blood is called hemolymph. It is made mostly of water and contains hormones, cells, and nutrients.

2 The sharp spines on the backs of *Pheidole drogon* ant soldiers contain muscle fibers that help the insects hold up their large heads.

3 Madagascar hissing cockroaches produce their famous hissing sounds by exhaling air through their breathing holes.

4 Human blood is red due to the red protein hemoglobin in most blood cells. Most insects lack hemoglobin, so their blood is either clear or tinted with a yellow or green pigment.

5 The veiny wings of a desert locust are 10 times thinner than a human hair. The veins conduct blood and help make the wings sturdy and perfect for flight.

6 The goat moth caterpillar has about 4,000 separate muscles in its body.

7 An insect's body is perforated by holes. The holes—called spiracles—are breathing pores and lead to tubes called tracheae inside the body.

8 The tiny brain of a fruit fly has about 300,000 brain cells. By comparison, the human brain has 100,000,000,000 brain cells.

BLOOD AND GUTS

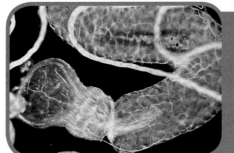

9 Termites have **bacteria** and other **tiny organisms** in their gut and digestive tract. These organisms help them **break down sugar** in wood.

10 Some insects, like Atlas moth pupae, can "hold their breath," taking in fresh air and expelling used air only once every several hours.

11 As a sucking insect **eats**, its head muscles work together like a **suction cup** to pull food into its digestive tract.

12 An insect's food is temporarily stored in an organ called a **crop**. The food remains in the crop until it can be **broken down** and its **nutrients** absorbed by the body.

13 Giant water bugs have a **powerful saliva** that helps them break down the insides of prey, such as fish and frogs.

14 Since a cockroach's brain does not control its breathing, the insect can survive for weeks without a head.

15 A **honeybee's brain** is about the size of a **sesame seed.** Scientists use electronic scanners to study insect brains.

a bluebottle fly feeding

❶ The parasitic wasp *Hymenoepimecis argyraphaga* lays its eggs inside orb-weaving spiders. When the larvae hatch from the eggs, they feed on the spider.

❷ The wasp larvae also direct the still living spider to spin a cocoon. Once the spider is finished, the larvae kill the arachnid and move into the cocoon.

❸ Atlas moth caterpillars are covered in fleshy spines coated with white wax that protects them from body-snatching insects.

❹ The young of a nematomorph hairworm develop inside grasshoppers and crickets until they mature into adults.

❺ The adult hairworms must live in water, so they force their insect hosts to jump into a lake or stream. The insect hosts drown as the hairworms move out.

❻ The larvae of Japanese lycaenid butterflies can mimic the odor of carpenter ants. This tricks the ants into adopting the larvae, ensuring their survival.

❼ *Glyptapanteles* wasp larvae develop inside geometrid moth caterpillars. When the larvae hatch from the eggs, they brainwash the caterpillars into being their bodyguards.

INSECT BODY SNATCHERS

A *Dinocampus* wasp inserts an egg into a ladybug, where the larva will develop and grow.

8 Larvae of the large decapitating fly mature inside a fire ant's head, where they feed on the ant's brain. When finished, the larvae pop the ant's head off.

9 A female jewel wasp injects chemicals into the brain of a cockroach, turning it into a zombie. The wasp then lays an egg inside the cockroach's abdomen, where it develops.

10 The wasp *Apocephalus borealis* lays its eggs inside a honeybee. A week later, up to 13 larvae hatch from the eggs and kill their host.

11 The infected honeybees behave strangely before dying. They abandon their hives and walk to a light source, where they sit and curl up.

12 A twisted-wing parasite mom never gets to see her larvae. That's because they devour their mother after developing inside her body.

13 A larva of the wasp *Dinocampus coccinellae* forces a ladybug to spin a cocoon for it—between her legs. The still living ladybug then protects the larva.

14 The brainworm *Dicrocoelium dendtriticum* invades the bodies of ants and takes over their minds. The brainworm forces the ants to climb blades of grass.

15 Eventually, the ants are eaten by grass-grazing animals, such as sheep. Once the ants are eaten, the brainworm emerges and settles inside the sheep's body.

15 DESTRUCTIVE FACTS ABOUT

1 Each year in the United States, lubber grasshopper nymphs descend on parks, gardens, and vegetable plots and consume plants.

2 In 2011, an army of termites invaded a bank in India, where they chomped through banknotes to a value of 10 million rupees. That's equivalent to U.S. $220,000.

3 During summers in the southeastern United Kingdom, thousands of small ermine moth caterpillars together weave huge webs of silk to protect themselves and their food plants from birds and other predators.

4 A giant swarm of grasshoppers infested Albuquerque, New Mexico, U.S.A., in 2014. The swarm was so dense that it appeared on the radar of the National Weather Service as rain.

5 In the 1990s, the brown marmorated stink bug hitched a ride from Asia to the United States in ship cargo. The bug has since spoiled fruit and vegetable crops in 41 states.

6 In the United States in 2015, the emerald ash borer—a beetle species—killed more than six million ash trees by digging burrows in the bark.

7 Asian long-horned beetles lay their eggs on the bark of trees such as maple and elm. When the larvae hatch, they tunnel into the bark—and ultimately destroy the wood.

INSECT INVASIONS

lubber grasshopper swarm
chewing on a plant

8 In 1848, a swarm of grasshoppers were devouring crops in Salt Lake Valley, Utah, U.S.A., when large flocks of seagulls arrived and gobbled up the insects.

9 In 1929, Mediterranean fruit flies found their way to Florida, U.S.A., where they infested 75 percent of the state's citrus trees. The National Guard was called to remove the pests.

10 Red flour beetles crawl into grain products, such as cereals and pasta, to feed and deposit their eggs. They ruin these products as a result.

11 In 1976, the aphid population in parts of England increased thanks largely to warmer temperatures. This attracted more than 23 billion ladybugs that fed on the aphids.

12 In 2011, millions of insects believed to be black maize beetles flocked to a beach in Argentina. The beetles may have taken refuge there from high winds.

13 In 2003, female mosquitoes spread the West Nile virus to about 6,000 people in the United States.

14 The Asian citrus psyllid—a plant louse—carries a bacterium that causes citrus trees, such as lemon trees, to become misshapen and turn green.

15 Gypsy moth larvae feed on more than 500 different plants. In swarms, they can destroy whole forests of trees such as oak.

73

1 AN ADULT FEMALE HUMMINGBIRD CAN EAT UP TO 2,000 INSECTS IN A SINGLE DAY. THIS INCLUDES MOSQUITOES, GNATS, BEES, FRUIT FLIES, CATERPILLARS, AND APHIDS.

2 Golden moles use their SHARP CLAWS to dig tunnels underground, where they feed on earthworms and INSECT LARVAE.

3 Northern cardinals eat 51 beetle species, 4 grasshopper species, and 12 hemipteran species, such as leafhoppers, cicadas, and aphids.

4 When a giant anteater raids a termite mound, it uses its CLAWS to tear open the nest and its two-foot (60-cm)-long sticky tongue to collect the insects.

5 THANKS TO AN ELASTIC TISSUE IN THEIR MOUTHS, CHAMELEONS shoot out their tongues AT TOP SPEED TO catch flies AND OTHER FAST-MOVING PREY.

25 FILLING FACTS ABOUT

6 Tenrecs hunt at night for small prey using their SUPER-SENSITIVE WHISKERS to detect VIBRATIONS made by moving animals such as beetles and ants.

7 SOME PLANTS GROW IN SOIL THAT'S LOW IN NUTRIENTS. TO MAKE UP FOR THESE CONDITIONS, THESE plants FEED ON nutrient-rich BODIES OF insects.

8 These insect-eating, or insectivorous, plants release DIGESTIVE ENZYMES that break down the insects' bodies.

10 The sundew plant has stalks covered in sticky blobs that look like dewdrops. When a fly zooms in for a drink, it gets stuck— and becomes lunch.

9 The Venus flytrap uses its clam-shaped leaves that are LINED WITH TINY HAIRS to trap insects to eat. When an insect touches the hairs, the LEAVES SLAM SHUT.

11 Pitcher plants trap insects in their cup-shaped leaves, which hold a POOL OF LIQUID and are rimmed with SLIPPERY NECTAR.

12 As an insect lands on the rim of a pitcher plant, it SLIPS and FALLS into the liquid below and drowns.

13

Hedgehogs use their **CURVED CLAWS** to dig for dirt-dwelling insects such as **BEETLES**, as well as earthworms and centipedes.

14 Insects such as mantids and wasps have **SHARP JAWS** that they use like **SHEARS** and **PLIERS** to cut and chew other insects.

15 Spined soldier bugs **DON'T CHEW** their meals. Instead, they use their long, **NEEDLELIKE** mouthparts to pierce their prey and suck up body fluids.

16 The three-banded armadillo HAS POOR EYESIGHT AND RELIES ON ITS sense of smell TO SNIFF OUT BEES, COCKROACHES, WASPS, AND OTHER INSECTS.

17 Aardvarks can **TRAVEL UP TO 19 MILES (30.6 KM)** each night, hunting for termites and ants.

INSECT-EATERS

18 Aardvarks have **SPECIAL ORGANS IN THEIR SNOUTS** that can detect the fine movements of the critters they like to eat.

19 Archerfish SQUIRT JETS OF WATER at land-dwelling insects, such as grasshoppers and butterflies, to KNOCK THEM into the water to eat.

20 ABOUT **70 PERCENT OF ALL BAT SPECIES** FEED ON INSECTS, SUCH AS BEETLES, MOSQUITOES, MOTHS, AND CRICKETS.

21 Insect-eating bats locate their food by making **CLICKING SOUNDS** that travel through the air to **BOUNCE BACK** from flying insects.

22 Unlike most bats, which make clicking sounds through their **MOUTHS**, horseshoe bats **USE THEIR NOSTRILS** to create sounds.

THE STAR-NOSED MOLE HAS A TENTACLE-LIKE NOSE COVERED WITH TINY SENSORS THAT HELP THE MOLE DETECT INSECTS AND EARTHWORMS **BENEATH THE GROUND.**

23 Horseshoe bats have a structure in their noses that **WORKS LIKE A MEGAPHONE** to amplify the sounds.

24

Woodpeckers use their beaks to **PECK HOLES** into wooden structures to find—and **GULP DOWN**—carpenter bee larvae.

25

15 GLOWING FACTS ABOUT

1 Some **fireflies, glowworms,** and **cockroaches** can produce their own light. This is called **bioluminescence** from the Greek word *bios*, meaning "**LIFE**," and the Latin word *lumen*, meaning "**LIGHT**."

2 Fireflies have special light cells in their bodies. When oxygen combines with a chemical called luciferin inside these cells, light is produced.

3 **Firefly larvae** can produce light—just like their adult counterparts. But unlike adults, which flash their lights, the larvae **produce short glows.**

4 Adult fireflies **flash their lights** in patterns. To create these patterns, **they control the amount of oxygen** that enters their light cells.

5 During the 1500s, bioluminescent **click beetles** of the genus *Pyrophorus* were used as **reading lamps** by native people of the West Indies.

6 *Pyrophorus* click beetles have two round bioluminescent organs on their upper thorax that glow like headlights.

7 New Zealand glowworm larvae live on **ceilings of caves.** To catch flying insects, they make **fishing lines** of silk that are **dotted with sticky, glowing globs.** The flying insects become stuck on these lines.

8 A glowworm larva takes up to 15 minutes to make a fishing line, and may produce as many as 25 lines a night.

INSECT LIGHTMAKERS

9 Railroad worms, a type of glowworm, produce green and red light. In fact, they are the only insects that produce red light.

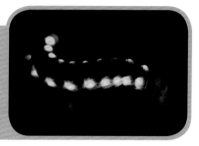

10 Male Jamaican click beetles produce a yellow-green or orange light to attract females. In response, female beetles produce a green or yellow light.

11 As a female New Zealand glowworm transforms into an adult, her body glow increases to attract a male partner.

12 A rare bioluminescent cockroach found in Ecuador has two glowing organs that look like eyes, as well as a third glowing organ on its side.

13 The glowing cockroach appears to mimic poisonous *Pyrophorus* beetles to keep predators away.

14 *Motyxia* millipedes—which are related to insects—glow to tell predators that they are toxic.

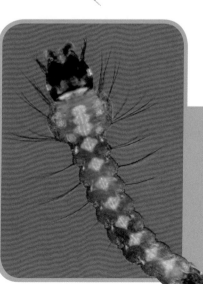

15 Scientists have transferred a light-producing protein found in some insects into mosquito larvae and into monkeys, cats, and mice to help them study how diseases are passed from one generation to the next.

light trails of Japanese fireflies

1
A group of adult butterflies can be called a **flutter**, a **kaleidoscope**, or a **swarm**.

2
Butterfly wings are clear. The tiny **scales** that cover their wings **reflect light**, causing us to see colors.

3
The muscles in a butterfly's thorax **move its wings** in a **figure-eight pattern** when flying.

4
Adult butterflies have **four wings**—two forewings and two hind wings.

5
There are about **14,000 known** butterfly **species**.

6
The butterfly **life cycle** involves complete metamorphosis, from **egg to larva**—a caterpillar—to **pupa**, or chrysalis, to **adult**.

7
Queen Alexandra's birdwing is the **world's largest butterfly species**. Its wings measure up to 11 inches (27.9 cm) from tip to tip.

8
The **smallest butterfly species** may be Sinai baton blue. Its wings measure about .37 inch (9.5 mm) from tip to tip. That's smaller than the diameter of an M&M.

9
The Sinai baton blue butterfly can be found only in **mountain regions of Sinai**, Egypt.

10
After a **monarch caterpillar** hatches, it **eats its eggshell**. It may also eat other monarch eggs it comes across.

11
Skipper butterflies are **fast fliers**. They can reach speeds of 37 miles an hour (59.5 km/h).

12
A butterfly uses the **receptors on its feet** to taste food.

13
Each butterfly species **lays its eggs** on a specific group of plants. For example, monarch butterflies lay eggs on **milkweed plants**, while black swallowtails prefer **dill plants**.

14
Before **laying her eggs**, a female butterfly must **identify the plant** to ensure her larvae can feed on it.

15
To identify a plant, the female butterfly **drums the plant surface** with her feet, causing the plant to **release chemicals** that are unique to the plant species.

16
Male butterflies often **drink from puddles** in muddy or sandy areas. The puddles are rich in **nutrients** and **salts** that help butterfly reproduction.

17
Butterflies fly best when the **air temperature** is between 75°F to 90°F (23.8°C to 32.2°C).

18
The painted-lady butterfly is the **most widespread butterfly** species. It can be found in the wild on all continents except South America and Antarctica.

19
The checkered skipper basks with its **wings flat and facing the sun**. This allows the skipper's dark wings to soak up as much heat as possible.

20
Butterfly ears were first identified in 1912. The ears are **membranes** on wings, legs, or the body that **vibrate** as sounds strike them.

21
Butterflies are found all **over the world**, even in the Arctic. The only place you won't spot one? **Antarctica**.

22
In 2015, scientists discovered an unusual *Lexias pardalis* butterfly. The individual had **right wings** typical of **females** of the species and **left wings** typical of **males**.

23
Female *Lexias pardalis* butterflies have **large wings** with **brown** and **yellow spots**. **Males** have **wings** that are **small** and dark with splashes of purple, blue, and green.

24
Julia butterflies in the Amazon rain forest **drink salty turtle tears**, which contain sodium—a **mineral** that's essential to their **diet**.

25
The **orange-tipped wings** of a *Hebomoia glaucippe* butterfly **contain a toxin** that's harmful to birds, ants, and other animals that try to eat it.

26
The **toxin** of the *Hebomoia glaucippe* butterfly is the **same** as one found in the **marble cone snail**.

27
Monarch butterflies migrate thousands of miles. Those populations that **travel farthest** have the **biggest** and **longest wings**. These wings help them **reduce drag**, a slowing force, as they fly.

the wing of a leopard lacewing butterfly

28
The chalkhill blue butterfly has **hairlike scales along its body** that give it a furry appearance.

29
The spring azure butterfly **lives for only a few days** after becoming an adult.

30
The Compton tortoiseshell butterfly **can live almost a year** after it becomes an adult.

31
Female butterflies of the *Redonda bordoni* species have **small wings** and **cannot fly.** They use their feet to move around.

32
Map butterflies lay their **eggs in columns** and only on the **stinging nettle plant.**

33
Orchard swallowtail larvae are **noisy eaters.** Their crunching sounds can be heard at night as they **feed on the leaves** of orange, tangerine, and lemon trees.

34
Swallowtail butterflies have **tail-like tips** on their hind wings.

35
If a predator grabs one of these tips, it **easily rips off.** This allows the swallowtail to escape.

36
Some predators have a difficult time spotting the adult **Indian leafwing butterfly.** At rest, the butterfly **looks like a dead leaf.**

37
Monarch butterflies usually fly between **40 and 100 miles (64.4 and 161 km) each day** when migrating.

38
Scientists once tracked a monarch butterfly that exceeded the average. It flew **265 miles (426 km)** in a single day.

39
The Rocky Mountain Apollo butterfly is named for **Apollo,** the Greek **god of music.**

40
The *Aristolochia* plant has a way to protect itself against **hungry butterfly** larvae. Its leaves **wither** around some eggs, causing them to fall to the ground.

41
In 2015, the **Tanana arctic butterfly** was spotted in Alaska, U.S.A. It had been **28 years** since the butterfly was last seen in the state.

42
The Tanana arctic butterfly first emerged during the **last ice age,** about 28,000 to 14,000 years ago.

43
Glasswing butterflies have almost totally **transparent wings.** This makes the butterflies **hard to see,** which **keeps them safe** from many predators.

44
The **88** and **89** butterflies are named for the **lines** and **dots** on their wings that form the patterns of these **two** numbers.

45
Butterflies and moths are **often confused.** Moths have **feathery** or **comblike antennae** while butterfly antennae are **club shaped.**

46
To keep *Heliconius* butterflies from depositing eggs on its **leaves** and **stems,** the *Passiflora* vine **produces egglike structures.** Butterflies assume the vine is **too crowded** and move away.

47
Once they have emerged from the chrysalis stage, female yucca giant skipper butterflies **do not eat.**

48
After Ross's metalmark butterfly **larvae hatch** from eggs, **wood ants** take them to underground nests and care for them.

49
Ross's metalmark caterpillars secrete **sugary honeydew** from glands in their hind legs. The **wood ants feed** on this honeydew.

50
Scientists believe that butterflies have been around for at least **65 million years.** This means they would have **fluttered around dinosaurs.**

50 Fluttering Facts About BUTTERFLIES

1 Female ermine moths are known for their speckled white wings and fluffy thorax and abdomen that resemble a weasel's white winter coat, or ermine.

2 Some insects have FALSE FACES to scare away predators. The back of a shield bug found in Singapore looks like the face of late singer ELVIS PRESLEY.

3 The BRIGHT COLOR of the shield bug's false face may be an important WEAPON—it suggests the bug is TOXIC.

4 When disturbed, the HICKORY HORNED DEVIL CATERPILLAR rears up and puts on a MENACING DISPLAY by tossing its horn-covered head from side to side.

5 PREDATORS that feed on young butterflies will likely avoid the PUPA of a darius butterfly. It looks just like a VIPER!

25 WONDERFUL FACTS

6 Macleay's spectre is a leaf-eater resembling a STICK WITH DEAD LEAVES.

7 The orchid mantis **disguises** itself as a **flower** while waiting for a pollinating bee to buzz in and be **devoured**.

8 Brazilian treehoppers have a **strange pronotum**—a part of their thorax that extends over the body and looks like **helicopter blades.**

9 The massive Goliath beetle weighs about the same as a large chicken egg. The beetle is named after the BIBLICAL GIANT GOLIATH, who was defeated by David and his SLINGSHOT.

10 As Goliath beetle larvae develop, they **GORGE ON HIGH-PROTEIN FOODS.** They can weigh up to 3.5 ounces (99 g). That's heavier than their adult form.

11 THE QUEEN AND WORKERS OF THE DRACULA ANT COLONY **CHEW HOLES IN THEIR LARVAE** AND **SUCK OUT THE BLOOD.** STRANGELY, THIS DOES NOT KILL THE LARVAE.

12 THE MALE ELEPHANT BEETLE'S TRIANGULAR PRONOTUM AND LARGE HORN—USED IN BATTLES AGAINST OTHER MALES—LOOK LIKE THE TRUNK AND EARS OF AN ELEPHANT.

13 The length of a female hose-nosed weevil's body is only .35 inch (8.9 mm), but its SNOUT IS TWICE AS LONG.

14 A male giraffe-necked weevil uses its superlength snout to FIGHT other males for the right to MATE with a female.

15 Stalk-eyed flies look odd. Their EYES REST ON ANTLERLIKE STALKS.

16 The peanut-head bug has a LARGE, HOLLOW DOME on its head that resembles an UNSHELLED PEANUT and helps the insect blend in with its environment.

17 IF PREDATORS MANAGE TO SEE THE PEANUT-HEAD BUG, THE INSECT UNFURLS ITS WINGS TO REVEAL TWO LARGE EYESPOTS, WHICH MAKES IT LOOK SCARY.

18 The GIANT WETA is a large cricketlike insect. Fully grown, it is about AS HEAVY AS THREE MICE.

ABOUT WEIRD INSECTS

19 The white witch moth has the LARGEST WINGSPAN of any known insect. It can measure almost 12 inches (30.5 cm) from wing tip to wing tip.

20  Most chalcid wasps have a NARROW WAIST and LARGE HIND LEGS, which they use to clasp on to butterfly pupae, where they lay their eggs.

21 Like their hummingbird namesake, hummingbird hawkmoths beat their wings so quickly that they MAKE A HUMMING SOUND.

22 As the hummingbird hawkmoth HOVERS above a flower, it extends its one-inch (2.5-cm)-long proboscis, which WORKS LIKE A FEEDING TUBE, to take up the nectar.

23 IN 2013, A PLANT-HOPPER WAS DISCOVERED IN SOUTH AMERICA WITH A TUFT OF HAIR SO THICK AND LONG THAT IT LOOKS LIKE IT BELONGS ON A TROLL DOLL.

24 The bizarre shapes of the PRONOTUM of treehoppers may have EVOLVED for camouflage, protection from predators, or mimicry.

25 Male luna moths have LONG, FEATHERED ANTENNAE, which they use to DETECT CHEMICALS emitted by female moths of the same species.

1 According to the International Union for Conservation of Nature (IUCN), **1,156 INSECT SPECIES** are **THREATENED** or at risk of **DYING OUT.**

2 High-speed traffic on roads is partly to blame for the gradual decline of HINE'S EMERALD DRAGONFLY populations. Passing cars kill thousands of these insects each year.

3 Apollo butterflies feed on *Corydalis* plants. In Afghanistan and Tajikistan, recent OVERGRAZING of these plants by SHEEP and GOATS has threatened the butterflies' survival.

4 Butterfly COLLECTORS once paid THOUSANDS OF DOLLARS for Queen Alexandra's birdwing butterflies. The butterflies were PLUCKED from their habitat, causing their numbers to drop.

5 Wallace's giant bee collects TREE RESIN to feed its young larvae. But LOGGING has reduced the number of trees and consequently the larvae's FOOD SUPPLY.

25 ALARMING FACTS ABOUT

6 Before the early 1900s, the Levuana moth could be found in Fiji. Since then, the MOTHS HAVE DISAPPEARED from this South Pacific island and may be extinct.

7 LEVUANA MOTH LARVAE FEED ON THE LEAVES OF **COCONUT PLANTS.** IN THE EARLY 20TH CENTURY, COCONUT GROWERS **DESTROYED THE MOTHS** TO PRESERVE THEIR CROPS.

8 Burying beetles feed their larvae animal carcasses. In the United States, recent habitat destruction has reduced the beetles' food supply, critically endangering the insects' survival.

9 Australian ant colonies build their nests in the soil beneath EUCALYPTUS TREES in Australia. When the trees are DESTROYED or REMOVED, ant numbers drop dramatically.

10 WILDFIRES are mostly to blame for the eucalyptus trees' destruction, but once a telephone company installing UNDERGROUND PHONE LINES removed many trees and endangered the ants' survival.

11 On the ISLAND OF MADEIRA off the coast of Portugal, the Madeira large white butterfly was last seen IN THE 1970s.

12 The Madeira large white **butterfly population** may have been **wiped out** by a **disease** that was passed on by an invasive butterfly species.

13 Since the 1920s, the Karner blue butterfly's **HABITAT** in the northeastern U.S. has been **REDUCED** by 95 PERCENT. This butterfly population is now low and sparse.

14

As **populations** of Karner blue butterflies have become separated from one another, **survival of the species** is threatened.

15 The Xerces blue butterfly once lived in SAND DUNES near San Francisco, California, U.S.A., but the butterflies **HAVEN'T BEEN SEEN** since the 1940s.

16 **INVASIVE ANTS** may have hitched rides with westbound **HUMAN TRAVELERS** and killed the Xerces blue butterfly population.

17 The fabulous green sphinx moth can be found on the Hawaiian island of KAUAI, where the species has been STRUGGLING TO STAY ALIVE.

18 **HURRICANE INIKI**, which struck the Hawaiian Islands in 1992, destroyed many of the moth's HOST PLANTS, which it needs to survive.

ENDANGERED INSECTS

19 **WATER POLLUTION** and **DROUGHT** have taken a toll on the glittering demoiselle—an African damselfly—which lays its eggs on plants floating in rivers and streams.

20

Between 2012 and 2013, about 45 percent of all **HONEYBEE HIVES** in the United States **VANISHED**. Many factors are responsible for the decline.

21 The VARROA MITE is one of the primary factors responsible for the honeybee decline. The mite sucks on BEE BLOOD, causing the bees to weaken and finally die.

22 THE BASKING MALACHITE IS A DAMSELFLY THAT LIVES AROUND ROCKY STREAMS IN SOUTH AFRICA. THERE MAY BE FEWER THAN 1,000 INDIVIDUALS LEFT IN THE WILD.

23 CATTLE from nearby FARMLANDS may be wandering into the malachite's habitat, TRAMPLING its eggs and killing off the population.

24 Rats threatened the survival of the Frégate Island giant **TENEBRIONID BEETLE** until the local government removed the rats in 2001.

25 TODAY, THE TENEBRIONID BEETLE FACES ANOTHER THREAT. A FUNGAL DISEASE HAS BEEN DESTROYING TREES IN WHICH THE BEETLE LIVES.

50 Breathtaking Facts About BEETLES

1
Beetles belong to the order Coleoptera, a term meaning "sheath wing."

2
Most beetles have two pairs of wings. The front pair, called elytra, are hard and stiff. They protect the beetle's hind wings, which are soft.

3
Flying beetles generally use their hind wings for flight. They occasionally flap their elytra to achieve an upward force called lift.

4
Some species, like the pie-dish beetle, have fused elytra and lack hind wings. These beetles cannot fly.

5
The largest known beetle is the Titan beetle. It grows up to 6.6 inches (16.7 cm) in length.

6
The Titan beetle has powerful jaws that can easily snap a pencil.

7
Despite their name, fireflies are not flies. They are beetles.

8
The smallest known beetle is Scydosella musawasensis.

9
Scydosella musawasensis is only .01 inch (.33 mm) long—as measured under a microscope.

10
A genus of scarab beetles, Termitotrox, lives in fungus gardens maintained by termites. It is not yet known how the two kinds of insects benefit each other.

11
In Cambodia in 2012, a Termitotrox beetle was discovered with wing-shaped outgrowths on the elytra. The species was named cupido for the wings of the Roman god of love, Cupid.

12
Years later, another Termitotrox beetle was found in the same region of Cambodia. The new beetle was given the species name venus after the Roman goddess of love.

13
When threatened by a bird or other predator, the bloody-nosed beetle releases a red, foul-tasting droplet from its mouth.

14
Ladybugs, which are a type of beetle, bleed from their legs when they are threatened.

15
There are almost 6,000 ladybug species. They vary in color and in pattern and number of dots on the body. Ladybugs and their spots can be orange, black, red, brown, or yellow.

16
American burying beetles are scavengers. The adults feed on organisms such as mice, birds, and snakes that have been killed by other animals.

17
If a dead animal is small, adult American burying beetles will feed on it themselves. If it's large, the beetles will bury it to provide food for their larvae.

18
To combat harmful bacteria found in dead animals, American burying beetles often carry tiny mites on their bodies. The mites eat the harmful bacteria.

19
Darkling beetles are nicknamed "clown beetles" because they stand on their heads when threatened.

20
If predators aren't intimidated by the headstand, darkling beetles will emit a foul-smelling fluid from their rears.

21
The rhinoceros beetle gets its name from the hornlike projections found on the heads of males. The males use these horns to fight rivals.

22
The strongest beetle is Onthophagus taurus. It can lift 1,141 times its own body weight. That's like an average adult man lifting six full double-decker buses!

84

23

Onthophagus taurus males use their superstrength to battle one another for a female beetle's attention.

24

In 2015, cave explorers in Serbia discovered a beetle species that looks like a spider. The species, named *Anthroherpon cylindricollie*, has long, spindly legs.

25

Waterlily beetles move their wings in a figure-eight pattern to zip across the water at speeds of 1.6 feet a second (50 cm/s).

26

Drilus beetle larvae kill and eat sleeping snails. After they're done eating, they move into the shells for a few weeks for shelter.

27

Dung beetles feed on feces, or poop, and are one of nature's recyclers.

28

Dung beetles can be rollers, forming dung balls and rolling them away from poop piles; tunnelers, which bury their dung under poop piles; or dwellers, which live inside the piles.

29

Agathidium vaderi, a type of slime mold beetle, is named after Darth Vader. Like the *Star Wars* villain, the beetle has a dark, shiny, helmet-like head.

30

To escape danger, tiger beetle larvae leap into the air, roll into a circle, and drop to the ground. The wind then blows them along.

31

With the wind's help, the tiger beetle larvae can turn 20 to 30 times a second, and travel for about 80 feet (24.4 m).

32

Female burying beetles that fight other insects for food put more effort into raising their young than non-fighting moms.

33

Panamanian golden tortoise beetles often appear gold but can change their color to red by controlling the amount of fluids in the layers of their wings.

34

To keep predators away, the larvae of golden tortoise beetles create fecal parasols, holding some of their poop over their heads like an umbrella.

35

Deltochilum valgum is the only known dung beetle to feed solely on millipedes. It often rips off the millipede's head before feeding on it.

36

Violin beetles are named for their flat, violin-like bodies. Their flattened shape helps them crawl in tight spaces where small prey may be nestled.

37

If threatened, violin beetles squirt their enemies with a painful acid.

38

Hide, or skin, beetles feed on the dead skin of animals—including humans.

39

Hide beetles have a powerful digestive enzyme that breaks down keratin, a protein that makes up fingernails, skin, and hair.

40

Natural history museums once used hide beetles to eat away fur and skin from the bones of animals that would be shown in an exhibition.

41

Red milkweed beetles have antennae sockets that divide each of their compound eyes. This gives the beetles four eyes instead of two.

42

Green dock beetles can walk up walls thanks to tiny hairs on their claws. The hairs fit into microscopic nooks and crannies in the walls.

43

The dock beetles can also walk on water. As the beetles move, the hairs trap air bubbles, which displace the water beneath them, creating buoyancy.

44

Beetle species in the Buprestidae family are called jewel beetles because they are brightly colored and have a metallic sheen.

45

Small hive beetles are known to invade the hives of African honeybees, eat the bees' honeycombs, and steal their honey.

46

The honey-loving hive beetles can detect chemicals released by bees when they are stressed or threatened. This helps the beetles locate the beehives.

47

If the African honeybees catch the hive beetle intruders, they imprison them in their hives.

48

Some dung beetles live in parts of South Africa where ground temperatures exceed 140°F (60°C).

49

To cool their legs, the beetles take a break from work and climb on top of their dung balls away from the hot ground.

50

In an experiment, dung beetles fitted with silicone booties took fewer breaks and did twice the amount of work than beetles without booties.

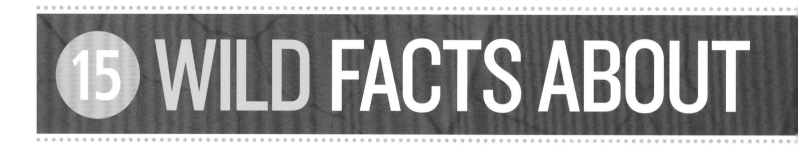

1 Conservationists suggest planting a butterfly garden to give the insects a safe haven to flutter in. You can create such a garden in your backyard.

2 Butterfly gardens should include brightly colored and strongly scented flowers, such as lantana and zinnia. These flowers attract butterflies and contain nectar, an insect food source.

3 In the United Kingdom, the Bumblebee Conservation Group has raised short-haired bumblebees in captivity since 2009. At the time, the bees were close to extinction.

4 In 2001, about 20 Lord Howe Island stick insects—a species believed extinct—were found on another South Pacific island. The insects were then raised in captivity and the population increased.

5 The U.S. Postal Service has regularly issued stamps featuring endangered butterflies to raise awareness about threats to the insects' survival.

6 To reduce the number of Hine's emerald dragonflies killed by cars, conservationists want to lower traffic speed limits in parts of Illinois, U.S.A., during summer months, when the adult dragonflies are active.

7 To monitor and protect all insect pollinators in Australia, conservationists there are asking the public to participate in the Wild Pollinator Count project.

butterflies feeding on wildflowers

INSECT CONSERVATION

8 People participating in the count are asked to record **pollinating bees, butterflies, wasps, flies, moths, beetles, thrips,** and **ants** in their local **community** and submit their findings to the **project organizers**.

9 To keep track of **ladybug populations** in North America, the **Lost Ladybug Project** asks citizens to photograph ladybugs **in the wild** and submit pictures to the organization's website.

10 In 2015, the U.S. government **pledged more than $3 million** to help boost the **monarch butterfly** population.

11 Monarch butterflies lay their eggs on **milkweed plants,** many of which have been **destroyed.** U.S. conservation groups are using the money to **sow milkweed seeds** to replenish milkweed plants.

12 In 2009, the U.K. Bumblebee Conservation Group reintroduced and raised **short-haired bumblebees** that were declared **extinct there in 2000.** Populations have survived in parts of England.

13 In 1998, the U.K. government **passed laws** that made it **illegal** to remove **stag beetles** from the wild and sell them to collectors. Stag beetle numbers rose as a result.

14 In 1983, officials in New Zealand **established a nature reserve** where Cromwell chafer beetles **can breed safely.**

15 In the Unites States, the National Wildlife Federation's **Garden for Wildlife Program** is helping local communities set up **small gardens** to attract all kinds of insects and other animals.

GLOSSARY

abdomen the rear main body section of an insect

algae simple plantlike organisms that contain a green pigment for photosynthesis but lack true stems, roots, and leaves

antennae body parts found near the front of an insect used for sensing objects and odors around them

aquatic relating to an organism that spends part or all of its life in water

arachnid an eight-legged organism, such as a spider, scorpion, mite, or tick. Arachnids belong to the class Arachnida.

arthropods a very large group of animals that each have an exoskeleton; includes insects, spiders, and crabs

bioluminescence the production of light by a living organism

camouflage an organism's ability to disguise its own appearance, often by using its coloring or body shape to blend in with its surroundings

caterpillar the larva of a butterfly or moth

chrysalis the name of the butterfly pupa

southern green stink bug

class a grouping together of organisms that have similar qualities. Insects are grouped in the class Insecta.

colony a group of the same kind of organism living or growing together

conservation the protection and care of natural resources, such as animals, plants, air, water, minerals, and land

courtship a behavior used by animals to attract each other for mating

defense a means by which an organism protects itself from attack or harm

elytra the hardened forewings, or wing covers, of beetles

endangered relating to a plant or animal that is found in such small numbers that it is at risk of becoming extinct

environment the natural features of a place, such as the weather, type of land, and plants that grow in it

exoskeleton the external skeleton that supports the body of an insect and other arthropods

eyespot a round marking that resembles an eye

feces the wastes that remain after food is digested. Insect feces are called frass.

forage to search widely for food

fossil the preserved remains or traces of an organism that lived a long time ago

butterfly with eyespots

fungus a simple organism with no leaves, flowers, or green pigment that reproduces by releasing spores. A fungus cannot make its own food and feeds on decaying plants and animals.

generation all individuals of a species that were born or hatched at about the same time

genus a group of species that are closely related to each other

gills the breathing organs of many water-dwelling animals, such as fish, crabs, tadpoles, and aquatic insects

grub the wormlike larva of an insect, especially a beetle

habitat a place in nature where an organism lives

hemoglobin a red protein in the blood of humans and other animals, including some insects, that carries oxygen to the cells

honeydew a sweet, sticky substance that is secreted by some insects

host an organism, such as a plant or insect, that another organism lives and feeds on

invasive relating to a species that is removed from its native habitat and introduced accidentally or on purpose to a new location, driving out a native species

larva (plural: larvae) the young stage of an insect's life. Larvae spend most of their time feeding.

luciferin a general term for a number of light-producing substances found in luminescent insects (such as fireflies). It is also found in plants and other animals and organisms.

mandibles the jaws of some insects, crustaceans, and centipedes, used mainly for tearing and chewing food, and for carrying objects

stag beetle

metamorphosis in insects, the process of changing from one stage in a life cycle to another

migration the seasonal movement of an organism from one location to another

mimicry the close resemblance of an organism to its surroundings or to another organism

molt to shed the outer covering of the body

mottled covered with spots or having colored areas

nectar a sweet liquid secreted by plants as food to attract animals that will benefit them

nymph the juvenile life stage in insects that undergo incomplete metamorphosis. Nymphs shed their skin, or molt, as they get bigger.

order a group of organisms that are closely related to one another. An order is a subdivision of a class.

pheromone an airborne chemical secreted by an insect or other animal that influences the behavior of other members of its species

pollen tiny grains produced by the male part of flowers that fertilize the future seeds of a plant of the same species

pollinators insects and other animals that carry pollen from one flower to another to help the plant produce new seeds

prey an animal that is hunted and eaten by other animals

proboscis the long, thin tube that forms part of the mouth of some insects

pronotum the hardened plate on top of the first segment of the thorax, just behind an insect's head

pupa the life stage of insects that undergo complete metamorphosis between the larva and adult in which the body breaks down and re-forms

sap a fluid that moves through the tissues of trees and other plants

scavenger an animal that feeds on dead or decaying matter

sedimentary rock a kind of rock formed by mineral particles, bits of older rock, and other natural materials that have been deposited over time by oceans, rivers, or glaciers

species a group of closely related organisms that can breed in nature and produce young

thorax the part of the body between the head and the abdomen where the legs and wings are found

toxic relating to a poisonous substance produced by some organisms

transparent allowing light to pass through

assassin bug

true bug an insect with piercing and sucking mouthparts that belongs in the order Hemiptera. This includes aphids, assassin bugs, cicadas, and giant water bugs.

tympanum a membrane that covers the hearing organ of some insects

KINDS OF INSECTS

To keep track of the many different living things on Earth, scientists classify them into groups that are based on traits, or characteristics, they share. The largest—and most diverse—group is called a kingdom. The smallest group, called a species, includes members that are very closely related and can mate with one another. Use the chart and information below to keep track of these groups—and discover how insects fit in.

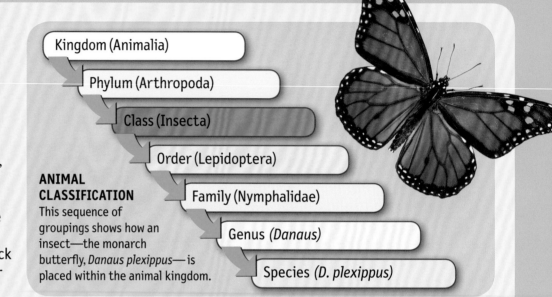

Kingdom (Animalia)
Phylum (Arthropoda)
Class (Insecta)
Order (Lepidoptera)
Family (Nymphalidae)
Genus (*Danaus*)
Species (*D. plexippus*)

ANIMAL CLASSIFICATION
This sequence of groupings shows how an insect—the monarch butterfly, *Danaus plexippus*—is placed within the animal kingdom.

SIMPLE METAMORPHOSIS

In those orders of insects listed opposite, each species has a life cycle that goes from egg, to nymph, to adult. The young, or nymphs, have wing pads in which the wings of the adults develop outside the exoskeleton.

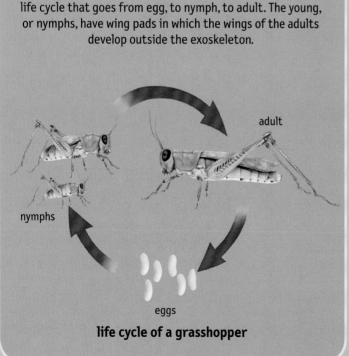

adult

nymphs

eggs

life cycle of a grasshopper

CLASSIFICATION

Within the class of animals Insecta are 28 orders, as listed here and on pages 92–93. Of these, 17 exhibit incomplete metamorphosis. Dark and light green backgrounds are used to distinguish the groupings.

Archaeognatha
Common name: bristletails
Characteristics:
- cylindrical, long body covered in tiny scales
- long antennae with many small segments
- three tail-like appendages on the abdomen
- wingless
- compound eyes meet in the middle of the head
- young insects look like miniature versions of the adults

Blattaria
Common names: cockroaches and termites
Characteristics:
- cockroaches have a flat, oval body, with the head hidden by pronotum, and long, slender antennae
- termites have an antlike body except the abdomen is not constricted at its base, short, thin antennae
- chewing mouthparts
- feet, called tarsi, have four or five segments
- young look like miniature versions of the adults

Dermaptera
Common name: earwigs
Characteristics:
- long, flat body
- appendages on the abdomen, called cerci, are made from hardened tissue
- short, hardened forewings and transparent hind wings
- chewing mouthparts
- antennae are average in size
- young look like miniature versions of the adults

Embiodea
Common name:
web spinners
Characteristics:
- long, cylinder-shaped body
- two pairs of wings in males; females are wingless
- short legs
- large front "feet," or tarsi, with silk glands
- young look like miniature versions of the adults

Ephemeroptera
Common name: mayflies
Characteristics:
- two pairs of transparent wings held above body
- hind wings are much smaller than forewings
- short, fine antennae
- mouthparts of adults are not used

- abdomen with 10 segments
- young adapted to live in water

Grylloblattodea
Common name:
rock crawlers
Characteristics:
- wingless
- appendages on the abdomen, called cerci, have eight or nine segments
- compound eyes are either small or absent
- leathery body
- antennae with 23 to 40 segments
- young look like miniature versions of the adults

Hemiptera
Common names: true bugs, aphids, and cicadas
Characteristics:
- two pairs of wings but some are wingless or have only forewings
- mouthparts formed as beaks for piercing and sucking food
- part of each forewing may be leather-like, others are entirely membranous
- wings are held at rest flat over body and overlap each other, or held rooflike over the body

- antennae have four or five segments, or are bristlelike in appearance
- adults of some groups have scent glands on the sides of the thorax
- young look like miniature versions of the adults

Mantodea
Common name:
praying mantids
Characteristics:
- long body
- forelegs have one or two rows of spines and are adapted for grasping prey
- two pairs of wings, which are used for flight; some are wingless
- movable, triangle-shaped head
- large, compound eyes
- young look like miniature versions of the adults

Odonata
Common names:
dragonflies and damselflies
Characteristics:
- long, slender abdomen
- two large, compound eyes and three simple eyes
- very small antennae
- chewing and biting mouthparts
- two pairs of transparent wings, sometimes colored
- young adapted to live in water

Orthoptera
Common names:
grasshoppers, katydids, crickets, and locusts
Characteristics:
- two pairs of wings
- straight body
- pronounced antennae
- forewings are straight, narrow, and have a parchment-like texture
- fanlike hind wings
- sound-producing organs in most males
- hind legs modified for jumping
- young look like miniature versions of the adults

Phasmida
Common names: walking sticks and leaf insects
Characteristics:
- two pairs of wings but some are wingless
- sticklike or leaflike
- long, slender legs
- long, slender abdomen
- leathery body
- long, slender antennae
- young look like miniature versions of the adults

Phthiraptera
Common name: lice
Characteristics:
- small, flat body
- wingless
- short, stubby antennae
- legs with hooked feet
- chewing and biting mouthparts
- young look like miniature versions of the adults

Plecoptera

Common name: stoneflies

Characteristics:

- long, flat, and soft body
- two pairs of wings that are usually held flat over the body at rest
- hind wings are wider than forewings
- long legs
- chewing and biting mouthparts
- antennae long and slender
- young adapted to live in water

Psocoptera

Common names: book lice and bark lice

Characteristics:

- small, soft-bodied with round, bulging head
- wingless, or two pairs of membranous wings held in rooflike position
- long antennae
- gnawing mouthparts
- scavengers
- young look like miniature versions of the adults

Thysanoptera

Common name: thrips

Characteristics:

- piercing-sucking mouthparts
- some have two pairs of narrow, fringed wings; others are wingless

---

- long, cylinder-shaped body
- adults are rarely longer than .07 inch (1.8 mm)
- legs end in bladder-like organs
- young look like miniature versions of the adults

Thysanura

Common name: silverfish

Characteristics:

- long, soft body
- small compound eyes; some species are eyeless
- wingless
- long antennae
- three tail-like appendages on the abdomen
- young insects look like miniature versions of the adults

Zoraptera

Common name: angel insects

Characteristics:

- minute insects, winged or wingless
- males have a pore on the head
- feet have two segments
- chewing mouthparts
- beadlike antennae with nine segments
- young look like miniature versions of the adults

COMPLETE METAMORPHOSIS

In the following 11 orders of insects, the life cycle has distinct stages. The wings of the adult develop inside the body of the young, or larva, under the exoskeleton.

pupa, known as chrysalis

adult

larva, known as caterpillar

eggs

life cycle of a butterfly

Coleoptera

Common names: beetles and weevils

Characteristics:

- forewings, called elytra, are thick and leathery or hard and brittle
- forewings meet in a straight line down the middle of the back and cover the hind wings
- chewing and biting mouthparts
- antennae are present and vary in size and shape
- compound eyes vary in size and shape
- young insects are commonly called grubs

Diptera

Common names: flies and mosquitoes

Characteristics:

- one pair of transparent wings
- hind wings are reduced to small, clublike structures
- sucking mouthparts; in mosquitoes mouthparts are adapted for piercing
- large, compound eyes
- short, simple antennae; some species have frilled or bushy antennae
- young insects are commonly called maggots

Hymenoptera

Common names: ants, bees, sawflies, and wasps

Characteristics:

- two pairs of transparent wings
- forewings are held to the smaller hind wings by tiny hooks
- females have a hard, tube-shaped organ for laying eggs or adapted for stinging
- chewing mouthparts except for bees, which have a tongue-like structure
- antennae with 10 or more segments
- young insects change dramatically as they develop into adults

Lepidoptera

Common names: moths, butterflies, and skippers

Characteristics:

- two pairs of wings; some moths are wingless
- wings are covered with tiny scales that overlap like roof shingles
- two large, compound eyes
- butterflies have clubbed antennae; male moths have large, feathery antennae while female moths have smaller antennae
- mouthparts are formed into a sucking tube
- young insects are often called caterpillars

Mecoptera

Common names: scorpionflies and hangingflies

Characteristics:

- slender body
- most species have two pairs of transparent wings that are similar in size; some species are wingless
- chewing mouthparts are at the bottom of a beak
- long, spindly legs with strong claws
- threadlike antennae about half as long as the insect's body
- young insects change dramatically as they develop into adults

Megaloptera

Common names: alderflies, dobsonflies, and fishflies

Characteristics:

- long, soft, flexible body
- long, threadlike antennae
- two pairs of transparent wings with many veins
- hind wings broader than front wings
- at rest, the wings are held rooflike over the body
- chewing and biting mouthparts
- young insects are commonly called hellgrammites

Neuroptera

Common names: lacewings, ant lions, owlflies, mantid-flies, and spoonwings

Characteristics:

- long, soft body
- two pairs of transparent wings that are equal in size and with many veins
- chewing and biting mouthparts
- large, compound eyes
- young insects change dramatically as they develop into adults

Raphidioptera

Common name: snakeflies

Characteristics:

- long body
- chewing and biting mouthparts
- front part of the thorax is long and snakelike
- forewings are similar in size to the hind wings
- wings are held rooflike over the abdomen when at rest
- young insects change dramatically as they develop into adults

Siphonaptera

Common name: fleas

Characteristics:

- small body, flattened side-to-side, usually less than 0.2 inch (5 mm) long
- piercing and sucking mouthparts
- large hind legs for jumping
- claws on feet for grasping hosts

- backward-pointing hairs and bristles on body
- young insects change dramatically as they develop into adults

Strepsiptera

Common name: twisted-wing parasites

Characteristics:

- males have forewings that are reduced to clublike structures
- males have large, fanlike hind wings
- males have antennae with four to seven segments
- males and females have reduced mouthparts
- females are wingless and legless, and have reduced mouthparts
- young insects change dramatically as they develop into adults

Trichoptera

Common name: caddisflies

Characteristics:

- small to medium-size bodies
- two pairs of wings that are covered in fine hairs
- wings form a roof over the abdomen when at rest
- reduced mouthparts
- long, slender antennae with many segments
- young insects change dramatically as they develop into adults

INDEX

Boldface indicates illustrations.

A
alderflies, 27, 93
angel insects, 92
ant lions, 93
ants, 12, 14–15, 17, 68, 93
  Allomerus decemarticulatus, 29
  Amazon, 29
  Australian colonies, 82
  Basiceros singularis, 29
  biomimicry of, 58, 59
  bulldog, 29
  carpenter, 14, 40, **40**, 66, 70
  Cataglyphis fortis, 30
  Cephalotes atratus, 21, **21**
  communication of, 58, 66, 67
  crazy, 14, 40
  dracula, 80
  driver, 29, 31, **31**, 48
  fire, 14, 39, 40, 65, **65**, 71
  garden, 14, 63
  harvester, 14, 23, 52, **52**
  honeypot, 15, **15**
  jumping, 15, 29
  leafcutter, 8, **8–9**, 14, 15, 23, 33
  meadow, 33
  Namib Desert dune, **34–35**, 35
  parasites and, 70, 71
  pavement, 31, **31**, 35, **35**
  societies of, 31, 48, 49, 62, 63
  trap-jaw, 14, 40
  velvet, 29
  weaver, 14, 23, 32, **32**
aphids, 26, **26**, 41, **41**, 52, 57, 73, **73**, 91
aquatic insects, **18**, 18–19, **19**, 34, 58, **58**
arachnids, 19, 22, 28, **28**, 46, 47
art and architecture, insect, 14, 32–33, **32–33**, 54–55, **54–55**, 64, **64–65**

B
backswimmer, 19
bark lice, 13, 92
bedbugs, 37, 38, **38**
bees, 16, **16**, 42–43, **42–43**, 62, 63, **64–65**, 93
  Anthophora pueblo, 43
  bumblebee, 35, **35**, 42, 50, 86, **86**, 87
  carpenter, 42, 75
  cuckoo, 28
  endangered, 82
  leafcutter, 42, 43, 45, **45**
  mason, 32
  pollination by, 50, **50–51**, 51
  Wallace's giant, 82

yellow jacket, 28
  See also honeybees
beetles, 13, 17, 27, 54, 60, 66, 84–85, 92
  arctic, 35
  ash borer, 72
  black maize, 73
  bombardier, 41, **41**
  burying, 29, 48, **48**, 49, **49**, 82, **82**, 84
  carrion, 48, **48**
  click, 29, 76, **76**, 77
  Cromwell chafer, 87
  desert, 35, **35**
  diving, 18, 19, **19**, 41, **41**, 58, 59
  dung, 30, **30**, 49, 57, 60, 84
  elephant, 80, **80**
  Epomis, 28
  fire-chaser, 17
  firefly, 28, 40, **40**, 54, 56, 66, 67, 76, **76–77**
  Goliath, 12, 80, **80**
  hibiscus harlequin, 48
  ironclad, 28, 41, **41**
  jewel, 85, **85**
  ladybug, 51, **51**, 64, **64**, 71, **71**
  leaf, 49, **49**
  long-horned, 60, 72, **72**
  Manticora, 29
  red flour, 73
  rhinoceros, 60, 84
  scarab, 54, 84
  stag, 87, **87**
  tenebrionid, 83, **83**
  tiger, 20, **20–21**, 21, 28
  Titan, 84, **84**
  tortoise, 41, 49, **49**
  violin, 85, **85**
  water, 36
  weevil, 56, 64, 81
  whirligig, 18, **18**, 21, **21**
biomimicry, 58–59, **58–59**
blood and guts of insects, 15, 68–69
blood-sucking insects, 9, 38–39, 69
bloodworms, 18
books. *See* stories with insects
brainworms, 71
bristletails, 90, 92
bugs
  ambush, 29
  assassin, 28, 29
  feather-legged, 29
  kissing, 38
  lace, 48, **48**, 49
  lovebug, 57
  milkweed, 41
  peanut-head, 81, **81**
  pirate, 29
  shield, 80
  soapberry, 56
  soldier, 75
  stink, 12, 29, 61, 72

sycamore lace, 48, **48**
  thorn, 24, **24**, 48, **48**, 57
  true bugs, 9, 12, 91
butterflies, 13, 16, 40, 55, 59, 66, 78–79, 86–87, 93
  Apollo, 79, 82, **82**
  blue, 25, **56**, 79
  blue morpho, 17, **17**
  comma, 53, **53**
  Compton tortoiseshell, 79
  darius, 80, **80**
  endangered, 82, 83, 86, 87
  images of, **56**, **78**, **79**, **86–87**
  Japanese lycaenid, 70
  Karner blue, 83, **83**
  Madeira large white, 82
  monarch, 21, **21**, 36, 52, 65, 66, 78, 79, 87
  owl, 25, **25**
  painted lady, 53, 78
  Queen Alexandra's birdwing, 78, 82
  skipper, 13, **13**, 93
  swallowtail, 25, 26–27, **26–27**, **56**, 79
  Xerces blue, 83
  See also caterpillars

C
caddisflies, 18, **18**, 32, **32**, 55, 93
camouflage, 24–25, 80, 81
  See also defense mechanisms
caterpillars, **7**, 12, **12**, 17, **17**, 27, 60, 70
  Apochima juglansiaria, 25
  blue butterfly, 25
  cabbage white butterfly, 40, **40**
  goat moth, 68
  hickory horned devil, 80, **80**
  jewel, 29
  masked birch, 67
  monarch, 36, **36**
  spicebush swallowtail, 25, **25**
  tent, 32, **32**, 63, **63**
  See also butterflies; moths
chiggers, 39, **39**
cicadas, 9, 27, **27**, 55, 91
classifications, 8, 9, 90–93
clothing and accessories, 54–55
cockroaches, 90
  anatomy of, 48, **48**, 68, **68**, 69, 77, **77**
  defenses of, 29, 66
  domino, 16
  foraging of, 31, **31**
  fossil of a, 44, **44**
  population of, 13, **13**
  senses and communication of, 16, 66, 68, **68**
commemorations for insects, 64–65
communication, 16, 58, 66–67, 75

conservation efforts, 82–83, 86–87
courting, 22, 56–57, 66
cousins of insects, 46–47, 77
crickets, 16, **16**, 41, **41**, 52, **52**, 54, 57, 60, 91

D
damselflies, 28, 48, 83, **83**, 91
defense mechanisms, 15, 29, 40–41, 72
  See also camouflage
diseases, 36, 37, 38, 39, 73
dobsonflies, 57, 93
dragonflies, 13, **13**, **16–17**, 17, 91
  darner, 28
  globe skimmer, 21, 52, **52**
  Hine's emerald, 82, **82**, 86
  jewelwing, 57
  Kirby's dropwing skimmer, 28
  nymphs, 18, **18**, 19
  prehistoric, 36, **36**, 45, **45**
  whitetail, 66

E
earwigs, 13, **13**, 29, 91
edible insects, 60–61, **60–61**
endangered insects, 82–83, 86, 87
extreme habitats of insects, 34–35

F
facts and figures about insects, 8–9, 12–13
fads and fashion, insect, **54**, 54–55, **55**
families of insects, 48, 48–49, **49**
festivals, insect, 64, 65
fictional insects, 22, 22–23, **23**
fleas, 12, 21, 39, **39**, 54, **54**, 93
flies, 17, **17**, 20, **20**, 27, 41, 55, 57, 71, 92
  balloon, 57
  blowfly, 39
  bluebottle, **68–69**
  brine, 19
  Canada thistle gall, 25, **25**
  fishfly, 93
  flesh, 51
  fruit, 16, 37, **37**, 57, 66, 68, **68**, 73
  horse, 20, **20**, 39, 52
  hover, 25, **25**
  robber, 28, 57
  scorpionfly, 56, 93
  screwworm, 38, **38**
  stalk-eyed, 81, **81**
  syrphid, 29
  tachnid, 29
  true flies, 12, **12**
food, 30–31, 60–61, 74–75
fossils, 36, **36**, 44, 45, **45**
froghoppers, 20, **20**, 33

G
genes, 36–37
glowing insects, 54, 55, 76–77, **76–77**
glowworms, 76, **76**, 77, **77**
gnats, 53
grasshoppers, 16, 60, 61, 91
  bow-winged, 57
  lubber, 72, **72–73**
  red-winged, 40, **40**
griffinflies, 44, **44**

H
habitats, 10–11, **10–11**, 14
hairworms, 70, **70**
hangingflies, 93
helpers, insect, 50–51
honeybees
  African, 29, 42, 85, **85**
  anatomy of, 69
  communication of, 52, 66, 67
  defenses of, 43, 71
  foraging of, 30, **30**
  hives of, 42, **42–43**, 66, 83, **83**
  jewelry icons of, 54, **54**
  mating of, 57
  migration of, 52, 53, **53**
  See also bees
hover flies, 25, **25**

I
insect-eating animals, **28**, 28–29, 40–41, **74**, 74–75, **75**
invasions by insects, 72–73

J
jewelry, 54, **54**, 55, **55**

K
katydids, 24, **24**, 25, **25**, 41, **41**, 66, 67, 91
kinds of insects, 90–93

L
lacewings, 24, 28, 29, 45, 93
ladybugs, 53, **53**, 73, **73**, 87
larvae, 27, 34, 60, 61, **61**, 70, 92
leaf insects, **6**, 24, **24**, 49, **49**, 91
lice, 13, 38, **38**, 73, 91, 92
life cycles, 26–27, 78, 90, **92**
locusts, 30, **30**, 31, **31**, **52–53**, 53, 68, 91

M
machines, insect-inspired, 58–59
mantidflies, 28, 93
mantises
  ambush tiger, 29
  devil's flower, 29
  leaf-litter, 24, **24**

orchid, 25, **25**, 80, **80**
  praying mantids, 28, 29, 48, 56, 64, **64**, 91
mating, 22, 56–57, 66
mayflies, 13, **13**, 18, **18**, 26, **26**, 57, 91
metamorphosis, 26, 27, 78, 89, 90, **90**, 92, **92**
Mexican jumping beans, 20, **20**
midges, 16, 18, 21, 34, **34**, 36
migration, 52–53, 78
milkweed bugs, 41
millipedes (arthropods), 28, 77, 85
mites (arachnids), 12, 29, 38, 39, **39**, 47, 83, **83**
mosquitoes, 12, 17, 19, 27, 38, 92
  arctic, 35, **35**
  courting by, 56
  disease from, 39, 73, **73**
  food of, 50, **50**
  images of, 38
moths, 13, 52, 53, 54, 93
  Atlas, 69, 70, **70**
  clothes, 31
  emperor, 60
  ermine, 72, **72**, 80, **80**
  flannel, 29
  ghost, 48, **48**
  gypsy, 37, 73, **73**
  hawkmoth, 29, 81, **81**
  Heliothis, 41, **41**
  Levuana, 82
  luna, 81
  peppered, 24, **24**
  silk, 56
  sphinx, 30, 83
  spider, 24
  tiger, 40, **40**, 41, 64, **64**
  white witch, 81
  yucca, 50
  See also caterpillars
movement of insects, 15, 18, 20–21, 52–53, 78
movies with insects, 22, **22–23**, 23

N
nymphs, 26, **26**, 29, 38, 90

O
owlflies, 93

P
parasites, 70–71, 93
plant-hoppers, 81, **81**
plants that eat insects, 51, **51**, 74, **74**
predators of insects, **28**, 28–29, 40–41, **74**, 74–75, **75**
prehistoric insects, 36, **36**, **44**, 44–45, **45**
pupa, 27, **27**, 92

R
robots, insect-inspired, 58–59, **58–59**
rock crawlers, 13, 91

S
sawflies, 30, **30**, 67, 93
Schmidt Pain Index, 39
scorpions (arachnids), 46, 47sculptures of insects, 64–65
sea skaters, 19
senses, 16–17
silverfish, 92
snakeflies, 93
societies, 14, 42, 62–63, **62–63**
spiders (arachnids), 22, 28, **28**, 46, 47
spittlebugs, 20, 33, **33**
spoonwings, 93
stick insects, 26, **26**, 29, 80, 86
stinging insects, 38–39
stoneflies, 18, **18**, 19, **19**, 30, **30**, 92
stories with insects, 22, **22**, 23, **23**

T
termites, 13, **13**, 26, 69, 90
  defenses of, 29, 40, **40**, 66
  food and, 31, 61, **61**, 72
  mounds of, 32, **32–33**, 33, 59, 74
  societies of, 62, **62–63**, 63, 84
thrips, 29, 38, 87, 92
ticks (arachnids), 12, 38, **38**, 47
treehoppers, 24, **24**, 37, **37**, 48, 67, 80, **80**, 81, **81**
twisted-wing parasites, 71, 93

W
walking stick insects, 24, **24**, 91
wasps, 31, **31**, 51, 64, 75, 93
  Ampulex dementor, 28
  Anoplius infuscatus, 29
  Apocephalus borealis, 71
  chalcid, 81
  cicada killer, 28
  common, 15
  Deuteragenia ossarium, 32
  Glyptapanteles, 70, **70**
  hornets, 28, 66
  Hymenoepimecis argyraphaga, 70
  ichneumonid, 29
  jewel, 29, 71, **71**
  mud dauber, 33, **33**
  paper, 33, 37, **37**, 57, 63, **63**
  tarantula hawk, 28, 39, 47
water bugs, 29, 49, **49**, 57, 69, **69**
water scorpions, 19
water striders, 18, **18**, 29, 56, 58, **58**
web spinners, 13, **13**, 91
weevils, 81, **81**, 92
weird insects, 80, **80–81**, 81
wetas, 81, **81**

RESOURCES

Websites
American Museum of Natural History Ology
amnh.org/explore/ology/search/(keyword)/insects

BioKids
biokids.umich.edu/critters/Insecta

BugGuide.Net about insects, spiders, and related groups
bugguide.net

DK Find Out!
dkfindout.com/us/animals-and-nature/insects

National Geographic Kids
kids.nationalgeographic.com/animals/hubs/insects

San Diego Zoo
kids.sandiegozoo.org/animals/insects

Tree of Life
tolweb.org

Books
de la Bédoyère, Camilla. *Bugs in the Backyard.* Firefly Books, 2016.

Discovery Channel. *Bugopedia: The Complete Guide to Everything Insect Plus Other Creepy Crawlies.* Discovery Channel, 2015.

Eaton, E. R., and **K. Kaufman.** *Kaufman Field Guide to Insects of North America.* Houghton Mifflin, 2007.

Gullan, P. J., and **P. S. Cranston.** *The Insects: An Outline of Entomology,* 5th ed. Wiley-Blackwell, 2014.

Johnson, N. F., and **C. A. Triplehorn.** *Borror and DeLong's Introduction to the Study of Insects,* 7th ed. Brooks Cole, 2004.

Murawski, Darlyne, and **Nancy Honovich.** *Ultimate Bugopedia: The Most Complete Bug Reference Ever.* National Geographic Kids, 2013.

Romero, Libby. *Ultimate Explorer Field Guide: Insects.* National Geographic Kids, 2017.

Romoser, W. S., and **J. G. Stoffolano.** *The Science of Entomology.* McGraw-Hill, 1998.

Simon, Seymour. *Insects.* HarperCollins, 2016.

Movies
Ants! Nature's Secret Power. Indigenius, 2004.

Life in the Undergrowth. BBC Home Entertainment, 2006.

The Magic School Bus: Bugs, Bugs, Bugs! Warner Home Video, 2009.

Monster Bug Wars, Seasons 1 and 2. Discovery, 2011 and 2012.

Wings of Life. Disney Nature, 2013.

CREDITS

PRODUCED FOR NATIONAL GEOGRAPHIC PARTNERS BY BENDER RICHARDSON WHITE

Since 1888, the National Geographic Society has funded more than 12,000 research, exploration, and preservation projects around the world. The Society receives funds from National Geographic Partners, LLC, funded in part by your purchase. A portion of the proceeds from this book supports this vital work.

NATIONAL GEOGRAPHIC and Yellow Border Design are trademarks of the National Geographic Society, used under license.

For more information, please visit nationalgeographic.com, call 1-800-647-5463, or write to the following address:

National Geographic Partners
1145 17th Street N.W.
Washington, D.C. 20036-4688 U.S.A.

Visit us online at nationalgeographic.com/books

For librarians and teachers: ngchildrensbooks.org

More for kids from National Geographic:
kids.nationalgeographic.com

For information about special discounts for bulk purchases, please contact National Geographic Books Special Sales: specialsales@natgeo.com

For rights or permissions inquiries, please contact National Geographic Books Subsidiary Rights: bookrights@natgeo.com

Hardcover ISBN: 978-1-4263-2993-7
Reinforced library binding ISBN: 978-1-4263-2994-4

The publisher would like to thank Professor Bill Lamp of the University of Maryland, College Park's Department of Entomology for his careful review of this book, and the project team of Bender Richardson White: Lionel Bender, editor/project manager; Nancy Honovich, author; Catherine Farley, copy editor/proofreader; Ben White, art director; Sharon Dortenzio, picture editor; Malcolm Smythe, designer; Kim Richardson, production manager; Amanda Rock, fact-checker; and Amron Gravett, indexer.

Printed in China
17/RRDS/1